MAGICKAL MERMAIDS

FLAVIA KATE PETERS

ROCKPOOL
PUBLISHING

A Rockpool book
PO Box 252
Summer Hill
NSW 2130
Australia
www.rockpoolpublishing.com.au
www.facebook.com/RockpoolPublishing
Follow us! 𝐟 ◎ rockpoolpublishing
Tag your images with #rockpoolpublishing

ISBN 978-1-925682-43-4

First published in 2019
Copyright text © Flavia Kate Peters, 2019
Copyright design © Rockpool Publishing 2019

Cover and internal design by Jessica Le, Rockpool Publishing
Editing by Lisa Macken
Cover image montage by Richard Crookes (Artwork *A Mermaid*, John William Waterhouse, 1900)
Typesetting by Envisage Information Technology, Chennai, India

 A catalogue record for this book is available from the National Library of Australia

Printed and bound in China
10 9 8 7 6 5 4 3 2 1

CONTENTS

Introduction v

1. Mermaid water magick 1

2. Mermaid connection magick. 29

3. Mermaid hair and mirror magick 55

4. Mermaid healing magick. 75

5. Mermaid moon magick 105

6. Spread the magick. 133

   Image credits. 143

   About the author. 144

INTRODUCTION

Imagine standing on the shore gazing out across a vast ocean as the water sparkles in the sunlight, dazzling you with the enticing colours of turquoise, blue and green. Your heart swells to the sound of the ebb and flow of the tide, and you try to push down the absolute desire you have to dive into the cool and very tempting waters. What is it that calls you so, to become immersed in the ocean? What urges you to become one with the seas? It's as though your very soul is seduced, or maybe even bewitched, for it is well known that humankind does not belong in the water. It is not our domain. But for those who hear the primordial call of the ocean the shoreline is a golden gateway into another kingdom, a watery sphere that has been a fascination here on dry land since ancient times.

Greek myths tell of how Poseidon, the Greek god of the sea, resided in the vast depths of the ocean in a golden palace that was adorned with corals, shells and jewels. Fish followed him wherever he swam, and he was guarded by two gigantic marine seas horses. Poseidon and Neptune, the Roman sea god equivalent, ruled the foaming waves by granting safe passage to seafarers or created ferocious storms, depending on their mood at the time.

Stories abound of a rich and glorious empire at its height of spiritual strength that was lost to the sea. The golden age of Atlantis remains a mystery, and the Temple of Poseidon, the Great Crystal of Atlantis and the original sphinx are said to be intact and sitting on an ocean bed, waiting to be uncovered.

Through the centuries sailors' relatings of an oceanic creature with the head and upper body of a beautiful woman and a huge fish tail in place of legs, appearing to them in the water, have been well documented. Tales abound of shipwrecks caused by the beauty and allurement of these mystical beings, who dive down deeply to uncover lost treasures.

It feels as though the fantastical underwater kingdom of the oceans and seas is leagues away from our life here on the surface, yet we can tap into its mysticism and mystery by connecting with the magickal world of the mermaids. Mermaids are made up of a high vibrating energy of light and resonate at a higher energy frequency than ours, which is why it is difficult sometimes for humans, who are of a heavier, denser energy, to see them. However, mermaids can freely appear to us by slowing down their vibrations, and can also be spotted as they frolic in the foamy seas during the magickal time of dusk, when the light is betwixt and between.

Mermaids are the witches of the seas, empowering goddesses of the water who reside on the astral plane, which is a magickal energetic frequency that we can connect with through meditation and spellwork and by raising our own vibrations. These alluring elementals help to ignite our own sensuality and seductive powers, whether we are male or female, and harness our natural powerful manifestation abilities.

As your heart opens at the hint of a magickal touch, you will uncover a world that has been hidden deep within. It is time to re-establish your magickal connection and swim through any blockages that have prevented you from tapping into your true potential.

Are you ready to dive into this book to explore the magickal realm of the oceans and its aquatic inhabitants and harness your own femme fatale?

As the energy of mermaids surrounds you, your magickal abilities will increase to support your dreams so you can reach for the stars. The watery world of the mermaids is poised ready to welcome you in as you discover the hidden depths of ancient magick that have been bubbling under the surface, and to uncover the mermaid within ...

CHAPTER 1

MERMAID WATER MAGICK

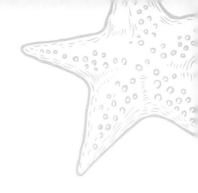

—\⁄⁄—

Whispers come upon the breeze,
through pretty shells and open seas.
But do you listen true and well?
Stop your rushing, heed the spell.
Pay attention, words await.
Mermaids now denote your fate.

—⁄⁄\\—

Did you know that it is the wild and alluring call of the mermaids that has enticed you to open up the pages of this book? Your thirst to connect with the oceanic kingdom and desire to bring a little elemental magick into your life is surging through you in response to the subtle messages the mermaids have been giving you lately. All the signs have been there, but did you take heed when a flash of turquoise caught your eye? Or how about when you were craving a bath or found yourself humming a simple lullaby? Perhaps you've been ignoring a desire to visit the ocean or have felt an anger rise within when you heard of another sea pollution news story. Chances are that your idea of heaven is to dive into deep clear waters of turquoise, to swim, float and splash around, because that's where you feel most at home.

Instead of getting caught up in the drama of life's challenges, the mermaids urge you to be still as stormy waves crash all around you and to simply listen. For in among the quietness you will find time for reflection and feel the pull of the ocean as the mermaids lure you back into their deep and uncharted territories, hook, line and sinker.

It's been a while since you swam with them, my friend. It is time to embrace the mermaid within and acknowledge your magickal powers; that is your birthright as a mermaid mystic.

The mermaids are calling you through the conch shell, the mobile phone of the seas. Did you ever visit the beach as a child and take home with you a seashell so that you could hear the sounds of the ocean whenever you held it to your ear? The shell was a direct line to the ocean itself that enabled you to listen to the echo of the waves crashing against the shore. No matter how far away from the sea you were it always worked, right? And you felt connected to the sea, to its interchangeable energy. But how did it work; how was it possible?

Well, you may not have realised at the time, but you were working with a supernatural and ancient source known as water magick.

As you swim through these pages you will discover how to harness your innate mermaid powers through the magick of water. Other mermaid secrets will be uncovered along the way. But first, let's look at some mermaids who might have inspired you to swim like a fish, pretend to sit on a rock and brush your long hair with a coral comb or to tie your feet together while in the bath and swish that tail.

- **The Little Mermaid**: probably the most famous and saddest mermaid tale of all was written by Hans Christian Andersen. How can we forget how she gave up everything for the love of a mortal man? So romantic, but at what cost? She could no longer speak let alone sing – her favourite pastime – and when her legs appeared in trade for her tongue it felt as though she was walking on razor blades. That would make any mermaid mystic wince! When she is rejected by her lover for another, the little mermaid is unable to return to the ocean and so she evaporates into sea foam. A lesson for us all!

- **Madison**: literally a fish out of water. When she decides to find the man she once saved from drowning as a little boy, she finds herself in the human world. Her curiosity and innate innocence lead to her arrest for nudity and to her falling in love with the man she once saved. *Splash* is a beautiful film starring the gorgeous Daryl Hannah, who is responsible for mermaid hair envy!

- **Miranda**: long before Madison swam across our screens, Hollywood featured Glynis Johns as a smart sea witch who charmed a man into taking her to see the sights of London and the human world. True to form, as an enchantress of the seas she seduced as many men as she could wrap her tail around!

- **Ariel**: bright red hair, fearless and headstrong can only mean one mermaid – and that's Hans Christian Andersen's *The Little Mermaid* turned Disney. Ariel is one sassy princess who knows her own mind, rocks a bikini top perfectly and has a fab wardrobe of stunning mer-gowns to boot! Her story is more than falling in love with Prince Eric, for she's an inspiration to the thousands who feel they don't fit in and teaches us to never back down and to keep smiling even in the face of fear.

- **The Starbucks mermaid**: this mermaid waves at each and every one of us from her shop front as an invitation to taste her wares. This is one mermaid who many have enjoyed wetting their whistle with, so to speak. The two-tailed mermaid is based on Melusine, a freshwater nymph and ancestor of the mediaeval French Lusignan royal family who was known to draw people to her – which has certainly worked well for Starbucks!

- **Real-life mermaids**: mermaiding is a growing trend for wannabe mermaids. Inspired by the little mermaid, Ariel, Madison and the others, there are mermaid fans all over the world who gather in oceans and swimming pools to dress up as mermaids in costumes with very beautiful, unique and realistic handcrafted tails. They dive, swim and play together and some help out in the ocean itself, looking after marine life as a real mermaid would. There are even mermaid holidays where you get given a tail, are taught how to swim like a mermaid underwater and receive a certificate at the end to say you are officially a mermaid. Fins up who wants one!

Mermaid memories

If you feel a deep connection with the ancient water-based civilisations of Atlantis or Lemuria, as well as being drawn to the magickal stars in the sky, there's a distinct possibility you have spent previous lifetimes in the water kingdom and as a mermaid. We have all had countless lifetimes, and not all in human form. For your soul's learning you can choose to incarnate wherever and into whomever you need to. Often a soul will feel most at home in a particular realm or frequency, and if you feel that you could originally hail from the magickal realms then that's where you will most likely have spent many lifetimes.

The energies in this earthly dimension are harsher than those in the magickal realms, which is why being here, on this planet, may seem quite hard for you now in this lifetime. If you feel that you have been a mermaid, then being on dry land may have caused you physical problems.

Perhaps you've experienced skin disorders such as eczema or psoriasis, or you've had walking difficulties in the past. Those who have had lifetimes as a mermaid are constantly thirsty and tend to drink a lot of water. They often suffer from extremely cold hands and feet no matter how warm the weather is, and yearn to be in or around the sea. Maybe you have a tattoo of a mermaid or another oceanic representation etched onto your body as a sub-conscious reminder of from where you came. You may have an enchanting singing voice or a natural allurement to seduce a potential lover at the beckon of a perfectly painted shellac fingernail!

Incarnated mermaids are easy to spot, for they often have hour-glass figures, wear their hair long and sometimes wavy, and suit the colours of blue, green, turquoise, silver and gold. Let's not forget the mermen, for they are the consort to the mermaid. Those mermen who have had previous lifetimes accompanying a mer-licious sea maiden are usually of a naturally athletic build and also sport long locks. Mermen do not have quite as much gravitas as mermaids, for it is the feminine who is and always has been the magickal personification of Mother Nature herself. However, mermen are great protectors of their consorts and of the oceanic kingdom. As a mermaid mystic you too are under the merman's protection; he will swim alongside you through any personal dark and deep waters to reveal the shining sunlight on the other side.

Mermaids were once respected and honoured by humankind. They were birthed from the water deities, the goddesses of the seas who ruled over and had the power to control the element of water, until they were forced into a retirement of myth and legend. But no matter how far they are pushed back into history these magickal beauties are still the sovereigns of the seas, tending to the aquatic inhabitants as well as our emotional subconsciousness.

Our ancestors worshipped the goddesses, the divine feminine. The mermaids call to us to remember, to remind us of where we are from, and they will always offer us a queenly reward when we focus reverent attention towards their existence. The energy we bestow upon them, through focus, invocation and honouring, will enforce their powers and enable them to return to the hearts and minds of humankind. For it was she who gave birth to the universe, the stars, the sun and the moon, the earth and the oceans, and it was from these primaeval waters that we emerged.

From the seas we are birthed, and to her we shall return …

Goddesses of the seas

Below is a list of a favourite few who are too powerful to be ignored and deserve to spring back to life through the foaming seas, swimming through our consciousness once more.

- **Tiamat**: this ocean goddess revered by the Sumerians, Assyrians, Akkadians and Babylonians predates all other deities. Through a sacred marriage between salt and fresh water, she gave birth to the first generation of creation beings: dragons, serpents and merpeople. Upon her death her body was used to form the land and sky, ensuring her influence over all beings that inhabit earth, including the seas.

- **Aphrodite** (Greek): Aphrodite was born out of sea foam when Kronos castrated his father Uranus and cast his member into the sea. Uranus' blood began to foam as it hit the water and transformed into the mermaid goddess of love, desire and beauty.

- **Amphitrite** (Greek): goddess of the ocean, queen of the sea and consort to the sea god himself, Poseidon. Known as the loud-moaning mother of fish, seals and dolphins, she has the power to still the winds and calm the seas.

- **Yemanjá** (Brazil): maternal goddess of the ocean who is the source of all waters. She protects boats travelling on the sea and grants safe passage; her colours are blue, silver and white. She assists with fertility, pregnancy and childbirth, and also heals mother issues and emotional wounds.

- **Sedna** (Inuit): Sedna was a beautiful maiden who was ostracised when she was impregnated by a wild animal. Her father took her out on the water to throw her overboard, but she clung to the side of the kayak so tight that he cut off her fingers. The fingers became sea creatures, and Sedna was immortalised as the goddess of the sea.

Through the erotic power of water rose the goddess, the giver of life. It is she who nurtured you within the warm waters of her womb, and it she who holds you afloat as you journey down the river of life back to the sea.

Ocean goddess love invocation

Tiamat, mother of mer
Allow the love within me to stir

Goddess of all beings of sea
Banish my fears, so I can be free
My heart has been broken, I suffered deep pain
I ask for your healing, for love I'll regain.

Aphrodite, divine feminine
Guide me to celebrate love from within
Of ocean born, you arose from foam
And love poured out from your very breastbone
To share of the essence of the divine
To bring about passion for all our kind

Amphitrite, mother of fish
Guide me to love and grant me my wish

Oh, to awaken the goddess within
To embrace my gifts of deep feminine

In your honour I sing and I dance
As I feel my heart open to love and romance

Yemanjá, mother of sea
Guide me to share the love within me

And now I see that the love within me
Reflects the pure divinity
Within my heart it doth reside
And shines forth, sparkling from my eyes

Sedna, goddess of the sea
Guide me to honour the love within me

As I grow stronger I am able to see
That it matters not that 'I' becomes 'we'
I focus on wisdom, on kindness to all
And the Inuit goddess ensures I am whole.

Ocean goddess of waters and sea
Thank you for the divine love within me.

Atargatis

There is one goddess out of all the rightfully crowned goddesses of the seas who is believed to be the inspiration to all the mermaid stories that have ever been told. She is the Assyrian goddess Atargatis.

Atargatis was the goddess of feminine powers, the moon and water. She was worshipped in ancient Assyria as an aspect of the universal mother, and her life-giving waters take us to the roots of mermaid stories and legends. Atargatis possessed the same elements as the mermaids have to this day, such as a beauty that cannot be hidden and the strong intuition of womanhood. Her story speaks of a broken heart and how her transition and transformation was supported by her connection with the element of emotions, that is, water.

Atargatis drowned herself in a lake after accidentally causing the death of her husband, Hadad. However, the waters could not hide her beauty and she was transformed into the first mermaid. Hers was the first mermaid story ever told and dates back over 4000 years. She guides all those who call out her name and are blinded by the fears of the deep, dark places within their selves.

Those deep-within places are but a reflection of the mysteries that are hidden in the depths of the ocean. We fear the unknown, and yet are fascinated by it. From the very first stories mankind has searched for the mythical mermaid, desiring to feel the pull of her allurement, to be enchanted in some way. While mermaids are said to cause the destruction of ships and the drowning of seafarers, there are also tales about mermaids rescuing sailors and taking them safely to shore. These tales represent the unpredictable ways of the oceans, which of course the mermaids are part of as the spirits of water.

Undines

Water cannot exist without its spirits; their energy is present within every drop of water on and within this planet. The spirits of water are called undines, which is the Latin word for wave. They refresh, clean and replenish your energy and can even be called upon to assist with working a little water magick. From lakes, rivers, streams, oceans and wells to the rain and puddles, each time you bathe or drink a glass of water you are communing with the undines on a subconscious level. Once you recognise this you can consciously work with them to utilise their magickal powers.

The spirits of the water come in various forms as guardians of lakes, rivers, pools, wells, oceans and seas. For instance:

- **Merfairies** are guardians of smaller bodies of water, such as lakes, pools, streams and rivers, as well as the plants and animals within the waters, which they tend to and nurture.

- **Water sprites** are guardians who play in the surf of fast-flowing rivers and play a vital purifying, healing role in the waters' ecosystems.

- **Delphinions** are guardians of sacred pools and wells who add healing frequencies to the waters.

- **Water nymphs**, also known as naiades, preside over bodies of fresh water such as fountains, brooks, waterfalls and wells.

- **Selkies** (meaning 'seal folk') are of Scottish origin; they shed their seal skin to take the form of a beautiful woman in order to lure young men into marriage. Some stories tell of their seal skin being stolen and the selkie being forced to marry. Often a selkie will miss the ocean so much she will eventually leave her husband to return to her natural habitat.

- **Sirens** are unbelievably beautiful women with wings and either a bird's body or a fish tail for their bottom half. They use their hypnotic singing voices and mystical beauty to lure ships towards dangerous rocks. They'd feast on the bodies of the dead sailors and were known to be bringers of death and destruction.

- **Nereids** are beautiful sea nymphs. Poseidon had 50 nereid daughters with his consort, Amphitrite; they were known to help sailors when they were in trouble.

- **Merrows** (of Irish origin) are half woman and half fish. They have thin webbing between their fingers and wear cloaks of seal skin and magickal red caps to assist their breathing under the water. To come ashore they abandon their clothing so as to appear mortal. They are forced to marry if their cloak and cap are stolen by the man who wishes to wed them. Like the selkies, merrows will eventually leave the land to return to the ocean.

- **Mermaids** are magickal guardians of the seas who nurture all that is alive and growing within bodies of water, which cover at least two-thirds of our planet.

Like all spirits of water mermaids reside on the astral plane, which is a magickal energetic frequency that you can connect with through your imagination, making wishes and opening your heart chakra, and through focused invocation and spellwork. Mermaid mystics find that the mermaids' magick is deep and nurturing because of their natural links with the goddess, the mother of the ocean, and the healing properties of water.

Mermaids remind you to follow the truth of your inner self, to awaken your deepest emotions and stimulate your compassion. This is because the etheric substance, that is, the spirit of water, is closely related to your feelings. Undines are in charge of the physical outpouring of the collective consciousness of human emotion. In other words, *the element of water is a representation of our emotions*. If it has been raining a lot, this is the undines mimicking the tears, grief and sadness of humankind. Whatever you give out and feel emotionally is replicated by the undines and given back to the world in physical form. Likewise, droughts and rainless periods reflect feelings and emotions that have been stuffed down and not allowed to come up to the surface.

You may be a very emotional person and have perhaps been accused of being over-emotional or too sensitive. Instead of worrying that the undines will replicate your flow of tears you can call upon the mermaids, the wards to the largest bodies of water on this planet, to assist in healing your deepest emotions. They are connected to you through your heart chakra and can feel your deepest hurts, as well as your love. The heart chakra stimulates balance, calmness and serenity, the same traits associated with water, and when aligned perfectly opens up a portal to the world of magick.

When your emotions are healed and your heart is cleared from blockages of grief, resentment and other lower energies caused by past hurts, you become more readily open to hear the voice and messages of the mermaids. Remember that sensitivity is a beautiful gift; it helps you to feel for others, to be both empathetic and sympathetic.

However, what you may wish to ask the undines is to assist you in being aware of whose feelings and emotions are affecting you. Are they yours, or are they the emotions of somebody else? The art is to observe how you are feeling and come to a realisation that you are not your feelings.

The mermaids can help you to understand whatever emotion comes up, and to discover where it has come from and why. You will find that, with the mermaid's help, you will soon be able to react to situations with a more masterful and balanced approach.

Water signs of the zodiac

Those born under the zodiac signs of Cancer, Scorpio and Pisces are usually receptive and extremely sensitive and have natural empathy and feel deeply. They desire for everyone to be as in love with beauty and romance as they are, and feel fulfilled when they are helping and nurturing others. Often they are loners and have a tendency to be self-indulgent or a bit moody; they are known to brood. Along with their alluring charm, water signs have the natural ability to see deeply into a situation and are in tune with their intuition. This is more so than for any other sign, for water sign people are in touch with their feelings and emotions, on which the element of water powerfully exerts its influence.

Water magick

The late and great scientist Dr Masaru Emoto dedicated his life's work to discovering the magick of water. His documented scientific evidence proves that water holds on to memory. Apologies if the words relating to 'science' made your beautiful mereyes glaze over, but it's great news that we have proof of the magick of water to present to any scoffers and naysayers out there.

In his exciting experiments Dr Emoto spoke words of love and positivity into a vessel of water. When he placed droplets from the same water under a microscope he was amazed to see perfectly and beautifully formed shapes that looked like very much like the formation of snowflakes when viewed in the same way. Into another vessel of water he spoke words that were fuelled with hatred and lower emotions. When he inspected the water this time it was a different story, for each droplet was twisted and contorted and not at all perfectly formed as previously.

The experiment proved that both bodies of water had responded to and remembered the vibrations of the words and feelings Dr Emoto had spoken. This means that water will retain the words we speak or emotions we are feeling and will respond accordingly, so it's extremely important to be careful what you say around water! It's a good idea to draw love hearts or ancient power symbols and those of protection on your drinking water bottles and kettle to ensure you consume water that is filled only with love and good intentions.

Likewise, be mindful of the words you speak to yourself. It's not only two-thirds of the planet that's covered in water; we ourselves are made up of a whopping 65 per cent of the wet stuff! This means that every time you look into the mirror and say something negative about yourself such as 'I'm too fat' or 'I'm looking terrible', guess what? Yep, you've got it – the water within you will hold on to the words and emotions of your damming exclamations and manifest it into physical reality. Yikes!

It really is a good idea to only speak words of love, encouragement and positivity about and to yourself. Make a special effort every day to tell yourself how wonderful, fit, healthy and successful you are, or whatever it is you wish to become, and the water within will naturally make it happen!

You can put your desires and intentions, through your words and feelings, into water to use for healing and magick. This is why you are encouraged to pray over water, for it will hold on to everything that is imbued into it. Saints and the great healers of old used water they infused with their prayers for healing, for they understood the magickal capacity of water. There are many bodies of healing waters all over the world such as the Chalice Well in Glastonbury, United Kingdom, the River Jordan and the Miraculous Spring of Our Lady Apparitions Grotto in Lourdes, France. Energy from prayers and wishes that have been directed towards a body of water grow stronger within the water itself, making it a wonderful elixir of desires, wants and promises.

Wishing wells have the same effect. When wishes are made into water an agreement is made with the water spirits who, in return for bringing about what the wish-maker desires, receives a nice shiny coin! Try this wishing well meditation:

Close your eyes and breathe in and out comfortably. See yourself surrounded by a ball of shimmering white reflective light so that only pure magickal energy can enter.

Breathe in love and breathe out peace; breathe in love and breathe out peace.

Imagine you are sitting in a beautiful soft glade surrounded by the strength of tall, majestic trees. Watch the soft sun slowly disappear from the horizon and bathe in the colours of the autumnal sunset, becoming drenched in the red and orange light that decorates the sky as you lie back upon the soft long grass and relax.

A westerly breeze picks up and gently caresses you as you watch the sylphs of the air dance round in circles with the swirl of the brown and copper leaves that fall all around you.

As you drift into a relaxed state, close your eyes as the autumn leaves continue to fall over and around you, covering you in a blanket of deep russet. Sink deeper and deeper into your thoughts and memories of the year gone by.

Were you all that you could have been? Did you take charge of your life? Did you allow others to put you down? Did you spend time trying to appease others?

As you track through any disappointments, imagine placing each hurt or regret onto a fallen leaf. Exhale deeply as you watch the fairies of the air blowing each leaf across the skies, releasing you from past pain and sorrows and the expectations of others; these now ride upon the changeable winds of autumn.

Eventually the leaf finally lands in its resting place, and as you reach to take up the leaf you've been chasing notice that standing before you is an ancient wishing well.

Carefully peer into the water of the well and hear the whispers echo from deep below, saying:

Faeries of water offer to heal,
Emotions of pain that hurt you to feel.
Cleanse and refresh, connecting to sea.
Dive into your heart, and swim so you're free.

The water will look so refreshing and appealing to you. As though you have been lured, seduced or enchanted in some way, you have an overwhelming desire to dive into the wishing well. Suddenly, as though your wish has been heard, you peer down into the well that has now become a sacred swirl of healing green water and immediately feel pure peace wash through your heart centre.

As you breathe this peace in, feel your heart chakra expand with love, like a balloon. As you exhale, feel the love circulating through your body.

Still breathing love in and out from your heart, see, sense or feel the sacred well of swirling green water grow enormously until you become a tiny version of yourself standing on the edge of the well. Dive in ...

The green water feels soothing, loving and very healing. You are swimming down ... down, down, down ... deeper and deeper, feeling nurtured, comfortable and safe. Down, down, down, deeper, deeper and deeper.

Three shimmering figures swim to meet you. One is blonde with a happy, friendly energy; one has red hair, wild with a passion flowing through her; and the third is dark and mysterious. They swim all around you, singing:

> We welcome you in, to the depths of your heart,
> This is where freedom truly doth start.
> Allow us to heal your sorrow and pain.
> Reveal us your wishes, do not ask in vain.
> Each one of us will grant a request.

Three in all, but which is the best?

You have been granted three magickal wishes. One wish is to be made with each of the three enchanting water nymphs, who are the wards of the well. Be careful as you make your wishes and direct them wisely, for each of these nymphs represents the magickal ingredient they can offer through their energy.

What wishes would you like to make? Which water nymph is best suited to bringing about your desire? Which wish would you make to the blonde nymph? How could the dark and mysterious water being assist you? Perhaps the wild energy of the red head could ignite something within.

You know your desires, so take your time to make your requests as you determine who is best to assist and with what at this time.

This is a wonderful and magickal moment as you make wishes to enable you to be the best you can be while ridding yourself of anything that has been holding you back.

Wishes granted, gifts received.
Pain amended, desires achieved.

Remember that it is a custom to give something in return and dig your hand deep into a pocket. As you pull your hand out, three shining crystals are revealed. Look at the colours and shape of each one in turn, and then hand the one that is the most suitable for each merfairy to her to say a heartfelt thank you.

You are pointed towards a tunnel, and you begin to swim up and up through a jewelled entrance of an iridescent rainbow of lights. Suddenly the fresh air hits you and you find yourself returned to full size and standing next to the wishing well.

With a smile and a new magickal energy surging through you, walk away towards your destiny without looking back, knowing that your wishes for your future have been granted and you are fully supported. Now say:

By the power of water, of ocean and sea.
With thanks I return, so might it be.

Take a deep breath in, feel the ground under your feet and open your eyes.

Welcome back!

CHAPTER 2

MERMAID CONNECTION MAGICK

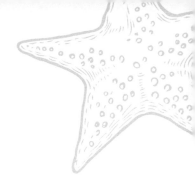

A magickal kingdom exists in my mind
Of wonder, enchantment and all of that kind
If I just close my eyes and count up to three
I see mermaids and dolphins who wait there for me.

Mermaids reside on the astral plane, which is a magickal energetic frequency that you can access easily through your imagination, wishes, invocation, meditation and spellwork. From their watery world mermaids reflect your greatest hopes, embody your deepest fears and assist in enhancing your natural magickal abilities to bring about your desires if you will but ask. The mermaids know that when you are in balance and harmony so too is the natural world, and so they wish for you to be your optimum best and will do everything in their power to add a sprinkle of very real magick into the lives of those who they inspire to be co-guardians of the oceans.

Mermaid altar

There is no better way to honour the mermaids than to create an altar that is dedicated to these frolicking goddesses of the seas, a sacred space where you can work some mermaid magick. This can be done by simply clearing a shelf in your bathroom or by covering a table in any room with a sparkly blue or turquoise cloth.

Try to ensure your altar is facing the magickal water direction of west if you can, and place a blue candle upon it. To represent the element of water place a chalice or goblet upon your altar, which you could fill with holy water from a sacred source or from a favourite stream or lake. Adorn the space with seashells, green, blue and turquoise crystals, dried seaweed and anything that you feel represents the ocean. Place figurines of mermaids, dolphins, whales, starfish and any other ocean treasures on the altar as you embrace the siren within. An altar is also a place for you to keep your magickal tools, such as a mirror, comb and anything else you may wish to use when creating mermaid magick.

Your altar is a shrine and dedication to the spirits of water, and is a focus point to connect with the magick of the mermaids. This means that every time you walk past the altar you will immediately be reminded of mermaids. The moment you think about them, their magickal energy will surround you. You may wish to specifically call upon them to enhance your psychic abilities, to heal your emotions or to bring about love, prosperity, abundance and healing into your life or another's.

Each of the four basic elements of water, fire, earth and air has its own specific magickal direction and time of day, which you can work to enhance the power of their properties for magickal purposes and connection. Exploring the forces of nature enables magickal practitioners to understand and work with the four elements and the elementals who are guardians of them.

1. **Water** governs our emotional well-being and our intuitive or psychic development. Engage with undines, water sprites and mermaids.

   Magickal direction: west.

   Magickal time: dusk.

   Magickal season: autumn.

   Candle: blue.

   Zodiac signs: Cancer, Scorpio and Pisces.

2. **Fire** is the motivating driving force, and gifts you strength and courage and fuels your passion for life. Salamanders, dragons and fire sprites can light up your life.

   Magickal direction: south.

   Magickal time: noon.

   Magickal season: summer.

   Candle: red.

   Zodiac signs: Aries, Leo and Sagittarius.

3. **Earth** maintains your logic and common sense, keeping you grounded and stable. Gnomes and dwarves hold this energy and are best called upon to reinforce earth power.

   Magickal direction: north.

   Magickal time: midnight.

   Magickal season: winter.

   Candle: brown or black.

   Zodiac signs: Capricorn, Taurus and Virgo.

4. **Air**: sylphs and fairies blow gifts of aspiration, inspiration, communication, clarity and creativity through your heart and mind.

   Magickal direction: east.

   Magickal time: dawn.

   Magickal season: spring.

   Candle: blue.

Zodiac signs: Libra, Aquarius and Gemini.

The direction of west is magickally connected with the element of water. Magickal practitioners and mermaid mystics connect with the magick of the mermaids by facing west, and understand that the best time to harness the powerful properties of mermaids is at the magickal time of dusk. The colour for candle magick is blue. Water is associated with autumn, where nature starts to turn within itself and you can reflect on where you have been and what you have done in the preceding months.

When you are ready to work with mermaid magick, face your altar and light the blue candle, preferably at dusk, and ask for that which you desire in the form of visualising what you wish for. As you see the item clearly in your mind or hold the intention of what you wish to come about, ask the mermaids to assist you through incantation, rhyme or a simple request that you can say out loud, silently or by singing.

This is how the mermaids grow and nurture the water plants and animals that are their ward. They see in their mind's eye the plants or beings as already being whole. Through their focus and intention they magickally manifest the plants and fish into the physical world, into our dimension. When you work in this way with the assistance of the mermaids, you too can bring your desires magickally into existence.

Connecting with mermaid energies

Once your altar is in place you will be ready to connect with the mermaids and to make mermaid magick. When the connection with the mermaids has been established you will find you become more aware of their presence every day, particularly whenever you use or are near water. Mermaids love to be acknowledged, so make sure you give thanks for the natural, cleansing, moist, life-force properties of water that we and our beloved planet benefit from and survive because of.

As your connection grows, the mermaids will continue to remind you to follow the truth of your inner self as they awaken your deepest emotions, stimulate your compassion and open your heart up to beauty, sensuality, pleasure, empowerment, magick and freedom. Dive deep within, and allow the magick to finally surface as you swim towards the truth of who you really are. Try the following mermaid connection spell.

Fill a bowl with water and place within it seashells and mermaid crystals such as:

- Aquamarine, which is known as the 'water of the sea' and is treasured by mermaids for its promises of eternal youth. Sailors often carried this precious gem for good luck and as protection from drowning.

- Blue lace agate, is a beautiful stone of peace that assists communication with the mermaids.

- Larimar, which has calming qualities and helps connection with the sea and oceanic mammals.

- Amazonite, which will take you deep within to connect with the ancient bodies of water.

Place the bowl on your altar. Face the altar in the magickal direction of west, light a blue candle and imagine a circle of protective light around you. Say:

Magickal mermaids I call upon you,
to surround and assist me in all that I do.
I invoke your magick, unite us as one.
By the power of water, we are blessed. It is done.

Blow the candle out and allow the smoke from the extinguished flame to wrap around you. Harness the empowering energy of the mermaids as you breathe in and out deeply, and feel every cell of your body vibrate with the magick and enchantment of the mermaids.

Dab the water with your power finger – the index finger of your dominant hand – and then gently touch your heart as you say:

I give thanks for this water so it may impart,
connection and healing to open my heart,
I connect with the mermaids, welcome unto me,
the power of rivers, of ocean and sea.

Masks

As you build a relationship with the mermaids they will encourage you to go much deeper than the surface, and to deeply examine yourself and your actions. Even though you may think you've got it all going on nicely, you may not be penetrating those old issues that lurk below the surface. It may appear to others and even to yourself that you are in control and are the master of your destiny, but if you aren't engaging in the deep, inner work of self-examination the chances are you are not aware of the real substance of who you are.

The desire to fit in with the world around can conceal the deep call of the soul, and all of us wear a mask to some degree. Most women, and some men too, will enhance their features by putting make-up on their face before stepping out of their front door. Clothing is also a mask. There are many uniforms you can don, including Goth, hippy, punk, casual, sporty, designer and business dress, that tell the world who you are. But does it really?

You can rely on the mermaids to swim to your rescue to reveal the truth of your inner reality, for they have watched and waited long enough for you to become your authentic self, to no longer cower behind the mask that has hidden the unique you.

So what's your disguise? Do you wear make-up and, if so, why? Is it to enhance your looks so that people will think you're more attractive than you think you are, or is it because you truly enjoy wearing it? It's so important to always be honest; it's the only way to break through the barriers in order to truly know yourself.

Which clothes do you prefer to wear? Maybe you like to look smart, to portray an air of good breeding, or perhaps you are a slave to fashion and have to be seen in the latest garments. But imagine how amazing it would be to get dressed every day in whatever clothing you felt would express who you are and how you feel. Think of how freeing it would be to act in the appropriate way to your true personality, how wonderful it would be to admit your genuine likes and dislikes and to act accordingly, never minding the judgements and opinions of others.

Our masks aren't always physical, as we often change our personalities to fit in with situations and other people. Many kind and sensitive souls change their ways so as not to be bullied or to appear weak.

Would-be mermaids often pretend to be in control when often they feel more comfortable just daydreaming and going with the flow. Do you wear a mask? Think about how you are with others. Do you change according to whose company you are in or depending on the situation? It is time to reveal the real you. Maybe you'd like to show the world who you really are but are scared of the reactions of others. What if you are rejected in some way? Are you brave enough to step out and expose your true nature?

Sometimes you will find you go out of your way to be the person others expect you to be. Is that so they don't think less of you, I wonder, or so that you don't let them and their expectations down?

Perhaps you're not ready to become unmasked and are reluctant to let your props go. Your disguise is your security and serves you well for now, but what would happen if you dropped the act? How would others react when they realised you aren't all you appeared to be: would you be treated differently?

Ask yourself these questions and do not be afraid to admit the truth in your answers. Only you can decide whether or not you continue to hide within a world of illusion or are brave enough to be your authentic self.

Try this incantation for removing your mask:

Now drop the mask, time to be free.
Mermaids reveal identity.
Dive down deeply to your core
Reaching to the seabed floor
And here you meet your inner mer
Feel your strength begin to stir
Shimmer, sparkle, swish your tail
You're here to shine, fatale female
Mermaids love those who are true.
Time to be the real you!

Mermaid makeover

Now that you have given yourself full permission to reveal your true mermaid self, let's look at some super sexy merstyles to spice up your life.

- **Bra**: from classic seashell bras to silicone bras with shiny scales, there are many stunning mermaid bras out there that have gone through rigorous tests and are approved for all kinds of mermaid activities!

- **Tail**: every mermaid needs a tail, and thankfully there are many realistic handcrafted tails out there that are not only stunningly beautiful, light and comfortable but also fit the purpose, including swimming in the ocean. All you need to do is to decide which colour monofin to choose. When a tail is less than practical, don't forget to wear fish-scale print leggings instead or a pair of sexy fishnet tights to channel your inner mer.

- **Make-up**: glamour up with ocean-themed, rainbow fish-esque creations on your face and body, and rock those turquoise-hued and purple eye shadows with a touch of iridescent highlighter and a slick of coral gloss for the ultimate mermaid look. Get those fishnet tights out again to stencil some scales on your face. Put the tights over your face and paint in shimmery green and blue eye shadow in areas that you wish to look scaly.

- **Glitter**: mermaid mystics just *love* to get all glittered up. Not only is it super pretty for face and body, but the particles reflect light at different angles and cause the surface of the skin to sparkle or shimmer in a beautiful spectrum of magentas, blues, purples, greens and turquoises – just like glistening mermaid scales! Remember to always use eco-glitter.

- **Accessories**: complete your mermaid look with sparkly jewellery, such as starfish earrings, a charm bracelet or a shell necklace. Don't forget to give your nails that shimmering sea look with fabulous mercolours and some added sparkle.

- **Crown**: from sparkling tiaras to jewelled coronets, no mermaid is complete without her crown. The moment you pop one on your head you will feel every inch the mermaid princess you are.

Go with the flow

When working with the magick of water a feminine energy is observed, for it is the receptive pure energy that naturally flows to you if you allow it that helps to manifest your desires.

Contrary to recent belief females are born to receive and males are born to give, to provide. Over the past few decades the roles of men and women have drawn closer together in similarity. Where men once went out to be the hunter gather, to provide food, safety and stability, women have now embraced that role as well. So instead of being in a natural receptive role the scales have been tipped as women strive to embrace the natural drive, focus and assertiveness of male tendencies, which goes against their very make-up. The masculine traits set a person up for success in business because their thoughts are purely focused on their goals; it's a natural progression for males. Women, on the other hand, can naturally think about more than one thing at a time, making it harder for them to be focused purely on one thing only at any given moment.

Empathy and nurturing are feminine traits that are most often associated with mermaids, who also identify with women's cravings to be deeply loved and to feel fulfilled. They naturally desire to be looked after, to just 'be', whereas men like to 'do'. Thus women have had to find their position of power by largely abandoning their feminine energy, thus losing their innate power. Women have been left feeling unbalanced, stressed and blocked, becoming rigid and losing their flow.

It's time to remember how to soften and to take the path of least resistance, to go with the flow. Sometimes it may be calm and serene and other times wild and turbulent, but always flowing forward just as a river does towards its destination.

Of course, men and women have access to both masculine and feminine energy, which is embraced when it is in balance. We are all born with one dominant form, either a male or a female energy, and should harness that which feels the most natural no matter what your physical form is.

Women have power and wisdom, connecting to their feelings and intuition more easily than someone who is predominantly masculine. However, it's important to tap into your divine femininity in order to align your body and heart so that you can easily hear these messages.

When you intentionally experience the natural pleasures your inner feminine desires you attract all that is your birthright, as a woman, to yourself. You will go with the natural flow of all things, and therefore will be able to receive all of the good you have been asking for for so long.

Everything is interconnected, and so when you embrace your feminine nature you not only nurture yourself but the oceans too, as well as the planet as a whole. Instead of trying to step into masculine shoes to earn a crust, draw success to yourself by harnessing your feminine energy – with help from the mermaids, of course!

Embrace your inner mermaid

Fill a bath tub with water. Light candles around it, add some essential oils and throw rose petals into the water. Splash about in the water and listen to its sound. Indulge in a glass of wine or a chocolate treat. As you relax in the warm water and flickering light, allow your five senses to become aroused and intentionally experience your sensuality.

Jewels such as a crystal necklace or one made from seashells will help you to connect with the natural abundant frequencies of the mermaids. Adorning yourself in riches such as pearls, crystals and other gorgeous jewellery will raise your self-esteem and leave you feeling rather fabulous, dahling!

See the beauty in everything around you by adorning your home with luscious fabrics, colourful decor and a little luxury. Express the mermaid within by adding your personal feminine touches to every room.

Dress the part: wear flowing skirts and dresses. Skip around in bare feet like the mermaid princess you are or rock those killer heels and that sheer lingerie piece as you channel your sexy side.

Experiment with your hair and make-up to give yourself a new look. Decide who and how you would love to be, being as bold as you like as you express yourself through this form of creative self-art.

The divine feminine craves creativity. It is through the womb that life is created, and it is this very life force energy that urges us to go create something. Painting, drawing, writing and gardening are wonderful ways to express your inner self. So, too, is cooking, crafting and even arranging social events. Once an idea is birthed the feminine energy of nurturing will bring it fully into being, and that includes your own ability to get in touch with your feminine side.

Sing as loudly and as often as you like. Feel yourself burst with delight as you sing your heart out in the shower, the car or the park as you find freedom and the natural expression of your voice and emotions. You will find it a liberating experience as you connect with the sounds of your soul.

Play a favourite piece of music and close your eyes. Allow the musical notes to take you away from your thoughts and lead you through a journey of sound. As you start to unwind and relax, breathe deeply in and out and become aware of how your body is responding. Start to slowly move your body in response to what you are hearing. Allow your body to move and become one with the music. Express the music through your movements and dance as sensually or as wildly as you like. Feel your feminine sexuality ooze through every part of your body as you dance through your senses and feel your body coming alive.

Mermaid music

Mermaids love the sound of music, and are well known for their beautiful strains of singing. The allurement of mermaid melodies is said to cause many a sailor to crash upon the rocks or send handsome young men to their deep ocean homes, due to the sweet siren sounds of the mesmerizing mermaid voices.

Mermaids understand how powerful music is as a manifestation tool. Music is actually part of the higher frequency invisible realm and has the power to elevate your thoughts and emotions. It works! Playing an upbeat pop song can make you feel happy and vibrant, and is great fun to listen to when getting glammed up for a night out. But for the mermaids music is much more than that, for they feel the music as they move to it and become one with every note as they work a little man-ifestation magick. They understand that as you focus on your dreams and sing, hum or chant about what you'd like to bring about, it is seeded by the high vibrational notes of the music and sent out across the ether to come into fruition.

Try this mermaid music manifestation:

- Play any type of music that you feel suits your mood.

- Move your body sensually to the music.

- Breathe it in deeply as you listen.

- Draw in the energy of each note.

- Hum or sing softly along with the music.

- Use your imagination to see your dream. Know it to be absolutely true and feel an excitement building up inside you.

- Feel gratitude, knowing that your dream is coming true.

Wishes and dreams come true when you truly feel joy and gratitude in your heart, and trust in your intuition as you take action to follow its guidance.

Dolphins

Your intuition provides much of the guidance and direction you seek. Because dolphins rely on their sixth sense, they also remind you to trust your feelings. Dolphins are highly evolved, intelligent and friendly beings whose love for humanity is profound. They live in the oceans and, like the mermaids, transcend time, space and physicality. They are here to help and support you as you swim towards radiant wholeness.

Mermaid mystics and many others are attracted to the playful and joyful energy that dolphins emit, because dolphins support humanity to make a shift from a world that is based on fear and struggle to one that is based on joy and love.

Dolphins are holders of ancient wisdom, and transmit planetary ascension energies as they swim and play in the ocean. If you're ever lucky enough to swim with dolphins they will bestow upon you their gifts of healing, deep growth and transformation. However, it's not always possible or even necessary to be in physical contact with these adorable ocean playmates to harness their energies. You can unite with their higher consciousness through your heart and imagination in meditation and telepathic communication to harness the balance, joy, wisdom and unconditional love they offer.

Mermaid connection meditation

You are standing on the shore, watching the ocean; watching the foam as it slides up the beach and then back again into the waters. Inhale the sea air, and become one with the waves as you breathe in and out deeply. Breathe in as the waves crash against the shore and exhale as the tide pulls back again.

As you look across the water you see a shimmering light dancing on the surface as the sun beams down upon it.

Feel that familiarity, that wanting, that needing, that absolute urge … You have to be a part of the ocean and your yearning is like never before.

Walk slowly down to the edge of the sea; let the waves gently lap your feet. Look down and see the sand in among your toes and step further forwards into the water, washing away the sand. Feel the coolness as you wade forward, through the water — further and further out until you realise you are floating, and so you stretch out your arms and turn onto your back. SPLASH! You look toward your feet floating horizontally in front of you. But instead of your feet you see a large, beautiful fish tail all the way down from your hips.

With a gasp, you recognise it immediately and move so that you can touch it with your hands, feel it, splash about with it.

See the colour, see how it shimmers. Dive in and out of the water. Do you remember the weight of it? And yet it is easy to move and you feel so powerful.

As you swim around you feel so liberated, so free with no restrictions. Feel your long flowing hair following your movements as you twist and turn. Look at the colour of your hair: isn't it beautiful? So soft and shiny.

You look down and see something that is a beautiful orange with dusty pink, and you dive down to take a closer look. It is a comb made of coral. You retrieve it, and with a mighty push you swim upwards to the surface.

With a gasp, you feel the warm sun on your face and swim across to a smooth rock that is jutting up out of the sea. With ease you hoist yourself up and make yourself comfortable on the rock. You pull your long, long hair round to your left side and start to pull the coral comb through it. Even though it is very tangled from the mixture of sea salt and the drying of the sun, you realise that you have missed this activity. Continue to comb your hair while basking in the golden warm light, and hum a simple tune.

After a while, you decide that the tangles won't come out completely and dive back into the sea. Immediately, your hair returns back to being soft and silky, waving around as you move

You continue to enjoy the freedom of floating around you, and then begin to sense something very familiar. Something is coming, something you are very connected with ...

You swim upwards toward the surface again and suddenly feel an object come beneath you. You are tossed high into the air and land back into the water. SPLASH!

With a gasp you look around to see what had caused such a thing, and you see a long, sleek grey nose practically touching yours. You pull back a bit and immediately recognise those dancing eyes; yes, it's your dolphin, your playmate and best friend. With a squeal of joy you fling your arms around him. He nods for you to get onto his back, and although he is slippery your tail grips magnificently.

Away you go: oh, what fun! As your dolphin glides through the water you breathe in the salty air, the colours, the surroundings and the spray. This is heaven, this is who you really are!

After a while the dolphin starts to swim towards the shore. Oh, but you don't want to go back; you want to stay! You jump off your friend and put your hand gently on his nose as you look deep into his eyes. His eyes are deep and penetrating, and full of ancient wisdom. Yes, you know what he is communicating to you: you must go back to human form. You agreed a long time ago to fulfil a mission that was much needed.

The dolphin assures you that your efforts aren't in vain and are much appreciated. He also reminds you that you can come back at any time, and that his and all of the magick of the ocean is with you at all times, supporting you. The secret, he winks, is to remember exactly who you really are.

You sigh a sigh of blissful awareness — and in a blink the dolphin is gone.

You step through the lapping waves and start to walk up the beach. Yes, you become suddenly aware that the fish tale has disappeared and you are back in human form.

CHAPTER 3

MERMAID HAIR AND MIRROR MAGICK

THE MERMAID ASKS FOR THE KING'S CHILD

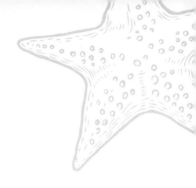

~⋅\⁄⋅~

Magick mirror help me see
The truth of whom I long to be
Unlock my heart, that is the key,
to reveal the mermaid, who is me.

~⁄\\~

A magick mirror is an ancient scrying tool in which the past, present and future is revealed, as well as all truths. For magick mirrors do not lie and therefore underline the basics of magick: that you may not always get the answer you want. However, you can be sure that whatever is revealed will always be for your highest good, and the mermaids will ensure your protection as you dive into the unknown to seek your destiny. A magick mirror is considered as a portal to the astral world when used in visualisation and spellwork, and the glass of the mirror represents the psychic properties of water, which reflect all that is seen and unseen.

While gazing into a handheld mirror the mermaid mystic understands the power of reflection, which is a sure way to connect with the enchantment of the mermaids in order to bring about your wishes and desires.

If you want to bring a certain action or outcome into being then your first task is to search for a beautiful handheld mirror that you feel will support you in your mermaid magickal work. To infuse it with mermaid energies, as well as stamping your own creative mark on it, you may wish to decorate it using shells, netting and crystals. This mirror is now ready to be part of your magickal tool collection, and is for your eyes only and not to be touched by any other. Keep it on your mermaid altar, or hide it away to bring out only when you are ready to work some mermaid magick.

Hair magick

When the time comes for you to use your magick mirror to manifest your desire into being, face west, light a blue candle and stare into the glass. As you gaze into the mirror, start to raise your magickal vibrations by continually brushing your hair.

Mermaids take pride in their appearance and use their long, flowing tresses to invoke their magickal manifestation abilities. Long hair is a mark of mermaids, particularly red or blonde hair, and is looked upon as being extremely powerful by magickal practitioners when used in spellwork.

To mermaids, cutting their hair short indicates grief or mourning. In fact, whenever anyone cuts their hair they are disempowering themselves in magickal terms. However, as hair holds the energy of the keeper, if one is filled with anger, jealousy and other lower emotions a haircut is in order to lose the negative energy it's holding. Often a break-up, disappointment or a failure will lead someone to desiring a haircut, and in this case will change their path of destiny.

Magickal practitioners recognise that hair possesses enchanted attributes that contain the essence of a person, and are careful not to let their own hair fall into the wrong hands, for negative spellwork could be cast against you if it does. Just one of your strands could give a person power over you. By burying a lock of someone's hair or shaving the whole head severs their magickal power and renders then powerless. Burn any of your cut hair and be careful with any fallout, particularly after brushing. It's a good idea to keep any hair that stays in your hairbrush or is pulled out with a comb to use for your own self-empowerment spells (see Chapter 5).

It's very easy to take on others' emotions just by touching their hair. If you create with hair as a profession, always imagine a bubble of light around you before and while you are working.

In ancient times women always braided their hair or wore it in a plait, which was often covered to protect their power. Never were they seen in public with loose hair, and only their husband could see or touch it; this is much like the customs of Muslim women today.

Mermaids know their magickal power is bound up in their hair, and the longer the hair the more it can affect others for it symbolises strength and powerful energy, which is associated with many ancient magickal rites and ceremonies.

The following are powerful hair styles:

- **Plait**: enhances psychic energy; the longer the plait the more powerful the woman.

- **Middle parting**: balances and harmonises the movement of energy.

- **Side parting**: when hair is combed to the left it represents feminine attributes; when combed to the right it represents the masculine.

- **Clean hair**: helps to focus and manifest your desired goal.

The following are powerful natural hair colours:

- **Black**: domineering and wayward energy. Sharp mindedness, magnetising and psychic. Powerful colour for rituals and spellwork. The colour of deep waters, black is associated with the element of water.

- **Red**: enhanced masculine energies of strength, enthusiasm and passion. Powerful magickal abilities, strong willpower and focus, perfect ingredients for spellwork. Red is associated with the element of fire.

- **Blonde**: peaceful and harmonising. Natural sea sirens. Powerful healers with communication and manifestation skills. The colour is believed to be born from the fairies. Blonde is associated with the element of air.

- **Brunette**: easy connection with nature. Sociable, friendly and logical. Natural magickal abilities and sexual magnetism. Centring and grounding multiplies their powers. Brown is associated with the element of earth.

- **Grey**: focused and close to oneness. Wise and understands what matters. Powerful magicians. Grey is associated with the element of spirit.

Allurement, seduction and beguilement are the traits of the mermaid; they ooze from the way they move with their long, flowing tresses, which represent their untamed sexuality and magickal abilities. Would-be mermaids can dye their hair the colour they desire, to become the mermaid they wish and know themselves to truly be. From streaks of purple and turquoise to full heads of green and teal, mermaids are showing up on the streets at every head turn. Aren't we lucky to be able to wear oceans of colour in our hair? Go back a couple of decades and green hair, which would have often been caused by over-chlorinated hair or a bad dye job, would've been covered up in shame by a head scarf or cut off to avoid major embarrassment!

It is evident that the magick of mermaid colours is spreading from vivid hues to the flawless blending trend. All mermaid styles can be as unique as you are, and if you've not yet dived in head first to experiment with some vibrant and luscious mercolours, then allow the following list of powerful mermaid colours to tempt you:

- **Blue:** has calming and cool, positive effects on the mind and body. It is a colour of depth and is associated with trust, loyalty, sincerity, wisdom, confidence, stability, faith and intelligence. The colour of both the sky and sea, blue brings feelings of peace, serenity and tranquillity.

- **Turquoise**: has cool, refreshing and calming attributes. It is associated with feminine energies, sophistication, wisdom, serenity, wholeness, creativity, emotional balance, good luck, spiritual grounding, friendship, love, joy, tranquillity, patience, intuition and loyalty.

- **Green**: the colour of nature and therefore of life. It is associated with growth, harmony, freshness, fertility and the environment. Green attracts prosperity and abundance, but be warned: it is also the colour of envy and jealousy.

- **Teal**: has the tranquillity of blue and the growth of green. It is associated with communication, balance and stability of emotions. Turquoise recharges you after stressful situations and heightens creativity, intuition, clarity, sensitivity and powers of perception.

- **Purple**: the colour of mystery and magick. It is associated with royalty, luxury, power and ambition and represents extravagance, wisdom, dignity, grandeur, devotion and independence.

Hair magick tip: if you wish to colour, cut or grow your hair it is wise to work with the phases of the moon, just as mermaids do. They understand how moon magick influences the ebb and flow of the tides of life, and how it also has a huge influence on the condition, length and growth of hair. (See Chapter 5 to work some powerful hair magick.)

When mermaid mystics brush their hair they understand that their glossy manes receive the energies of whatever they are thinking at the time. It is useful, therefore, to focus upon your heart's desire when combing or brushing your hair. By doing so, you will send out into the ether the energy and powers needed to implement your desires. And through the ritual of brushing your hair while performing mirror magick, you will double the power of your spellwork.

Mirror magick affirmations

If you wish to bring about something, gaze into a mirror and start to invoke your power by brushing your hair while stating positive affirmations, intentions and desires. You can do this silently or out loud, and as you do open up your clairvoyant abilities by seeing all that you wish for in your mind's eye by imagining it all in the reflection staring back at you.

For instance, you may wish to affirm that you are in good health so you repeat:

MAGICKAL MERMAIDS

I see myself as healed and whole. I see myself as healed and whole.

Say it, believe it to be so and see yourself as healed and whole in the mirror.

If you would like to attract beauty to and around you, then it is important to see yourself as that very energy. As you brush your hair, gaze into the glass and affirm that it is so by saying repeatedly:

I am beautiful. I am beautiful.

Say it, believe it to be so and see yourself as beautiful in the mirror. To bring about your desires, such as success, say:

I am successful in all ways. I am successful in all ways.

Say it, believe it to be so and see yourself as successful in the mirror.

Mirror magick works powerfully in cooperation with your own belief, and will reflect back to you all that you believe in and all that you believe you see. It's exactly how the mermaids work when they add their touch of magick to the oceans and seas and all bodies of water. They imagine a water plant wholly grown, and see it in their mind's eye. As they hold that image and believe in it, it manifests into existence and is done.

Mirror magick exercise

This exercise will help you to connect with your mermaid self. You will need:

- long-handled mirror
- shells, feathers, beads
- glass of water
- seashells or crystals
- CD of the sound of waves (optional)
- blue candle
- hair brush

Choose a mirror, preferably with a handle you can hold on to as you gaze into the glass. This is to be your very own magick mirror, so you may like to decorate it with shells, feathers and colourful beads. Make it personal and special to you, as this is your gateway to connect with the psychic powers of water and the magick of the mermaids.

Prepare your ritual space by placing around you the glass of water and seashells or crystals such as aquamarine. Begin playing your music. Imagine a circle of protective light all around you. Face west and light the candle, in honour of the water spirits. Pick up your magick mirror, watch your reflection as you brush your hair with long, slow strokes and say:

Magick mirror help me see
the truth of whom I long to be
Unlock my heart that is the key,
to reveal the mermaid, who is me!

Feeling relaxed but continuing to brush, drift into a world of mer for a while as you hum a simple tune.

Imagine you are sitting on a large rock in the middle of the ocean. Inhale the sea air and listen to the crash of the waves against the stone you sit upon. As you brush your hair in slow sweeps you look down to see that, instead of legs, you have a beautiful fish tail all the way down from your hips. Look at it in detail; touch it. You may wish to dive into the clear, cool waters and splash about. Have fun, play and enjoy being a mermaid again.

Rest and relax as you harness empowering energy, which spreads through you, resonating with and vibrating in every cell with the magick, seduction, beauty and enchantment of the mermaids.

When you wish to return to dry land, take a look again in the mirror and say:

By the power of water, of ocean and sea
With thanks I return, so might it be.

Drink the glass of water, blessing it before you do so.

Mermaid guides

At some point everyone with a magickal heart has wished they had someone to help them through a difficult time, or to grant them a wish at the flick of a wand. It is in the enchanted realm of the astral plane that the mermaids, who have magickal powers and can bring good fortune to those who ask and deserve their help, reside. From here the mermaid guides watch over and protect their wards.

Now that you have connected with the magick of the mermaids and your inner merself, you are ready to invite in your mermaid guide. Anyone with an open heart or of a sensitive nature has their very own mermaid, who is waiting to be called upon. Once you have connected with your mermaid guide she can be called on to help you bring magick into your everyday life, as well as heal your emotional well-being and pour upon you the abundance and prosperity that is your birthright as you live out your days here on the physical earth plane.

The mermaids remind us that our imagination bridges our physical reality with the astral world, and is the key that unlocks the world of magick. They are waiting to reveal the true beauty and power of your inner self, and can assist you with magickal solutions and insights if you will but ask. This powerful meditation, the through-the-magick-mirror meditation, will invite in the magick of your very own mermaid guide to help you to unlock your true potential. Close your eyes and take three deep breaths, in and out.

Imagine you are sitting in front of a beautiful ornate gold mirror that's decorated with seashells at the mermaid magickal time of dusk.

Peer into the magick mirror and set your intentions by saying:

Mirror, mirror give me sight.
Show me shadows through the light.
Reveal the one who guards me well
That we might meet through cast of spell

Accept, I shall, new power in me,
Mirror, mirror let me see.

Light a blue candle and gaze into the flame. Breathe deeply, in and out, through your heart centre. Feel the warmth of your heart as it expands to an overwhelming, immense feeling of love. This is the time to call upon the mermaids who are ready to transform you into your glorious real self.

Gaze into the mirror and watch as the flame dances in its reflection. Say:

A magickal kingdom exists through my heart
Sacred flames glow show me where to start

I'll look in the mirror, for I'm longing to see
My mermaid guide, to appear to me.

The light flickers across the shadows in the glass until it takes shape and transforms into a resplendent mermaid – your mermaid guide! She radiates out before you, smiling, and the love from your heart expands towards hers. She is indeed beautiful and you notice her shimmering tail, her long and decorated hair and the jewels she wears, including the powerful crystal wand she holds in her hand. She exudes magick and a power that contains deep and ancient wisdom, while overflowing with a depth of kindness. Take your time to see her, to really look at her. Feel her warmth and love, and remember that on a deep cellular level you know her. Take your time to reconnect with your mermaid guide.

Once you have familiarised yourselves, you hear sweet singing ring through you:

Mermaid magick takes you far,
so make your wish upon a star.
Believe these things will come to you,
for this will make your wish come true.
Now close your eyes, count up to three,
I'll wave my wand; now wait and see.

This is your opportunity to ask your mermaid guide for any magickal assistance you may need. Once you have made your wishes she will invite you to peer into the magick mirror. Your mermaid guide promises that whenever she turns up she will listen, that she will always lend a sympathetic ear, and you can be sure she will get to the depths of the problem.

As she works with you, allow her to unearth hidden emotions that have been festering, such as jealousy or anger. These lower agitations will be exposed and you will have no choice but to learn how to deal with them. But don't be alarmed, for your mermaid guide is with you every step of the way. She encourages you to dig deep, and get to the bottom of the feelings that have prevented you from receiving all that you have been desiring. Be strong, be brave and be comforted to know that your mermaid guide only has your highest interest at heart, as she shatters any illusions that have blinded you from the truth.

Empowerment is her gift. She offers you the chance for new life, new beginnings and changes through the magickal act of transcendence.

Your mermaid guide lifts her magnificent crystal wand, which streams a powerful light through into your heart, clearing any blockages and opening you to a receptive level.

Feel the magick and breathe it in. Allow it to surge through every part of your very being. Feel the dream happening; feel the knowingness of your wishes being granted and coming true. Magick surrounds and fills you as you stand strong in your own power, which has been fully awakened.

Nod your head with a beautiful smile toward your mermaid guide as an acknowledgement, and remind yourself to leave a small offering for her in return.

As you softly blow out the candle flame watch your mermaid guide swim away. Although you can no longer see her you can feel her strong presence as magick continues to pulse through you, and the warmth in your heart continues to glow.

Slowly bring yourself back, take a stretch and open your eyes, knowing that you have made a connection with your mermaid guide. She will always hear your call as she listens to your requests through her magickal seashell and through the love in your heart, whenever you need her magickal assistance.

CHAPTER 4

MERMAID HEALING MAGICK

HANS ANDERSEN'S FAIRY TALES

CHARLES ROBINSON PECLD 1897

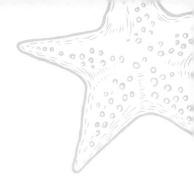

_-\\I/_

_Magickal mermaids offer to heal,
emotions so strong that hurt you to feel.
Cleansing, refreshing, connecting to sea,
dive deeply within to heal and be free._

_-/I\\-_

The element of water is symbolic for spiritual rebirth and renewal, puri-
fication and regeneration. It is the source from which we are birthed,
the amniotic waters of the womb. The healing power of the mermaids
enables you to let go of your ego self so you can throw caution to the
wind and dive deeply down within to uncover the core of who you truly
are. Transformation is the gift of the mermaids; they enhance our wisdom and perception as we learn to go with the flow.

Mermaid healing is deep and nurturing and can uncover blocks to
fertility, pregnancy and childbirth, as well as to heal mother/father issues
and wounds. Mermaids work primarily with emotions and tune in well

to your sensitivities. Most illnesses are made manifest into the physical from your thoughts, worries and fears. The mermaids understand this, and are able to dive right in to search for and uncover the root of the problem in order to soothe and wash away the negative emotions connected with any disease.

Mermaids seek out sensitivity and encourage you to tap into your emotional feelings. They wash away old hurts, uncover your natural psychic abilities and enhance prophetic dreams that are ready to emerge. If your energy is affected by negative thoughts, doubts and worries, allow the mermaids to wash them away as they release the emotions that are draining your natural vitality and positive outlook.

Positive tide healing

The energy of water is considered as receptive, so when you are feeling down and low imagine you are standing at the seashore. As the tide pulls back it takes away from you all the negative aspects you are feeling. As the tide draws the ocean towards you, so it gifts you with positivity and prosperity. Be open to receive and ready to flow naturally with life.

Seashells

Many magickal healers work with the healing properties of crystals, but often underestimate the healing and protection abilities of seashells.

Our ancestors turned to nature for their power objects and recognised that seashells are imbued with spiritual energies that we can harness for our own use in spellwork and for healing.

Seashells come in many shapes and sizes and play a big part in biological and geological beach processes. Culturally, people have collected shells for millennia. West Africans used cowrie shells as currency, and indigenous people throughout the world have used seashells for lamps, cutting tools, decoration and jewellery. Beachcombers can spend hours searching for shells of interest to them, for seashells have always been a fascination to mankind and are also beautiful keepsakes as reminders of the seaside. Perhaps you enjoyed collecting shells in a colourful plastic bucket as a child. Maybe you still have a collection, or have just two or three in your bathroom to give you that seaside feeling, as shells have a powerful and direct connection with the energy of the ocean itself.

Of course, the main purpose of a shell is to provide a hard, protective outer layer for the soft-bodied sea animal that lives within it, or as part of its body. These are often coiled to make a safe place for them to hide their bodies, and are quite thick and tough to protect them should they be thrown about by the waves. Made up of proteins and calcium carbonate, shells are exoskeletons of molluscs (soft-bodied invertebrates) such as sea snails, scallops, clams, oysters, periwinkles, cockles, mussels and many others.

Shells from the ocean have a direct connection with the energy of the sea animals they house and of the salty, cleansing properties of the sea herself. Seashells have been imbued with the strength and life-giving power of sunlight and the magickal effects of the moon and the stars. You can then see why seashells are powerful, reviving and effective tools when it comes to using them for mermaid healing work. Each species of shell has specific patterns and markings and varies in shape and size, depending on which sea creature it has evolved from. Below is a list of some common but super powerful shells that are perfect for seashell healing:

- Auger: tall, spindly cone up to 3 cm in length. Common anywhere with muddy sediments.
- Baltic tellin: plump, almost circular shell 2.5 cm in length. Pink, yellow, purple or white.
- Banded wedge: wedge-shaped shell up to 4 cm in length in shiny white, yellow, purple or brown.
- Blunt gaper: large shell up to 7.5 cm in length. Colours range from white to dark brown. Common on sandy, muddy or stony shores.
- Cockle: fan-shaped shell radiating up to 5 cm across. Found in estuaries and sandy bays.

- Limpet: Conical grey or white shell up to 6 cm high with ridges. Found on rocky shores.
- Oyster: oval- or pear-shaped shell up to 11 cm across. The two halves of the shell are very different – one is smooth and flat; the other is rough and concave.
- Periwinkle: black or grey conical shell up to 5 cm in height. Found particularly on rocky coasts.
- Piddock: large, brittle shell up to 12 cm in length with ridges. Dull white or grey.
- Whelk: yellow-brown spiralling shell up to 10 cm high and 6 cm wide.
- Grey top: small whorled shell 1.7 cm across. Grey or light yellow with brown or purple streaks.
- Thick top: turban-like spire up to 3 cm in height in green, grey or black.
- Thin tellin: brittle, flattened shell up to 3 cm in length in shades of pink and yellow. Common on sandy shores.
- Painted top: conical violet/pink and brown streaked shell up to 3 cm high. Very common on seaweed-covered rocky shores.

Taking a shellfie

You may feel drawn to visit a beach to collect a few shells to assist you in your healing work. Before you do so, ask the mermaids out loud or quietly in your mind for permission to take from the beach, and then wander around to see which shells call to you. Allow your heart to be open, and then retrieve in love and gratitude any shells that have glinted or gleamed up at you.

Here is a simple but welcome incantation you can use when asking permission from the mermaids before taking anything from the beach. You can do this out aloud or silently by saying:

> *Dear mermaids, 'tis you that I wish to beseech,*
> *for my heart desires a gift from the beach.*
> *Please grant me permission, release unto me,*
> *this beautiful treasure of ocean and sea.*

You may wish to make a promise to the mermaids in exchange for the gift you took, such as to send healing to all of the inhabitants of the ocean or to collect any litter you find along the seashore.

Cleansing and recharging seashells

Shells taken from the ocean need little ritual preparation, however, if your shells were bought from a store or haven't been used in a very long time they will benefit from being cleansed and recharged. Like crystals, seashells can attract and absorb all kinds of vibrations, both positive and negative, so it is crucial that you cleanse them prior to use to remove any negativity and to keep their vibration and healing energy high.

There are various methods of cleansing seashells; it is a matter of personal preference. Seashells are sacred and precious and should always be treated with the utmost care.

Take your shells to a natural source of clean, fresh water such as the sea or a stream and place or hold them in the water. You can also hold them under running water from a tap. If you bless the water the blessings will infuse the properties of the water with love, thus benefiting the seashells and the healing. You can also rub a few drops of holy water, such as water from the Chalice Well in Glastonbury, on your seashells to purify them and lift their vibrations.

Never dry your crystals with a towel. Instead, allow them to dry naturally.

To cleanse and recharge your shells in one go, place them in a bowl of water mixed with sea salt to soak overnight under the direct light of a full moon. If being recharged through the day, set them outside or on a windowsill to drink in the light of the sun.

Meditating with seashells

Meditation can rejuvenate both body and mind, instil inner peace, awaken insights and grants us access to different dimensions. Seashells are a wonderful tool mermaid mystics use to help induce and enhance a meditative state of peace and tranquillity and to tap into the energies of the ocean. To meditate with seashells:

- Take a seashell and hold it gently in your hands.
- Focus your attention on the seashell.
- Notice its beauty, its shape, form and colour.
- Close your eyes and become aware of your breathing.
- Breathe in deeply from your abdomen and give a long, slow exhale, blowing deliberately through your mouth.
- As you exhale, feel any tension in your body dissolving.
- Continue breathing in this way until your mind is free from any thoughts.
- Allow yourself to sink deeper and deeper into a meditative state.
- Imagine that you are becoming part of the seashell.
- Allow your energy to merge with that of the seashell, becoming aware that you both have the same spirit running through your vital life force energy.

- Allow yourself to enter your shell and explore its magickal kingdom.
- Feel your energy field expanding and filling with the energies of the ocean.
- Remain in your blissful, meditative state for as long as you wish.
- When you are ready to return, become aware of your body and your contact with the earth. Gently move your fingers and toes and notice your surroundings.
- Take a deep breath in and slowly open your eyes.
- Thank the spirit of the seashell and the guardianship of the mermaids.

Healing with seashells: chakras

Seashells are wonderful at helping clear and cleanse the chakra energy points found in your subtle body in which *prana*, or life force energy, flows through. Those who are attuned to energy healing systems such as reiki work to heal, cleanse and balance the chakras for themselves and their clients, to bring about wholeness and balance.

The seven main chakras are aligned centrally though the body. Each chakra has its own colour (etheric) that represents its own metaphysical energy. If a chakra is out of alignment due to negativity, fearful thoughts, beliefs and doubts surrounding what the chakra represents it will cause imbalance, which can affect you on every level including manifesting physical dis-ease. For example, worrying about money could cause your base chakra to become stagnant, because this is the energy point that represents security and material needs. Fearful thoughts and a belief in deficiency will cause this chakra to become unbalanced, which could manifest into physical pain or dis-ease such as lower back problems.

When chakras are stuck like this it can be beneficial to release the stagnant energy by using seashells, and to encourage the flow of vital and fresh energy back into the body. It can be a very relaxing and powerful healing experience. To help you in your healing work the shells should be placed, as crystals would be, on the various parts of the body that need healing. The etheric of each chakra is as follows:

- **red**: base or root chakra; safety, survival, security, grounding, material needs

- **orange**: sacral chakra; emotions, creativity, sexuality, flow

- **yellow**: solar plexus chakra; confidence, personal power, will

- **green**: heart chakra; love, empathy, compassion, relationships

- **blue**: throat chakra; truth, creative expression, communication

- **indigo**: third eye chakra; intuition, extrasensory perception, inner wisdom
- **purple**: crown chakra; universal connection, spirituality, consciousness

Crown Chakra

Third Eye Chakra

Throat Chakra

Heart Chakra

Solar Plexus Chakra

Sacral Chakra

Root Chakra

For chakra healing and balancing:

- Create a safe and quiet sacred space.

- Light a blue candle and play soft ambient music, preferably with the sounds of the ocean.

- Lie down and place a shell on each of your chakra points.

- Visualise the shell drawing up any negative energy that each chakra may have been holding.

- Breathe deeply in and out as the shell energy drenches each point with its healing and cleansing properties.

- Relax and rest as the shells restore you to a place of balance and wholeness.

Mermaid Healing Energy System® attunement

Using and working with seashells is an effective way of bringing the soothing qualities of water into your healing work – but you can super-charge your healing sessions to an even greater level once you are attuned to the Mermaid Energy Healing System®, which will assist you with secret and unique healing energies. Usually I initiate the attunement myself during my mermaid magick workshops, although special mermaid permission has been granted for this sacred initiation to be shared within these pages to connect you to the mermaids' healing abilities and to enhance your own.

The sacred shell symbol is for your eyes only, mermaid mystic, and to be used with reverence and sanctity. Draw the sacred shell symbol into your palm chakras before a mermaid healing session. Visualise it in your mind's eye as you use your intention and focus to let the mermaid healing energy flow through your hands during a healing session. The healing energies and guidance from the mermaids will pass through your hands to where healing is needed.

The sacred shell symbol can be drawn literally or in your mind's eye onto each palm of your hands.

Draw, clockwise, a large, closed circle nine times. When the ninth circle is completed, start on the tenth circle by pulling your finger away from your palm. While your finger is still turning clockwise, draw more circles that gradually get smaller and smaller while continuing to pull away from your palm, thus forming a spiral, in order to form the etheric shell. See in your mind's eye the shell glow in a golden colour.

Stop the circles you have been drawing at the thirteenth, when you have come to the final point at the top of the shell. You can also picture in your mind's eye the golden shell coming from your third eye before and during a treatment.

It is very easy to use the energy of the mermaids during a healing session, as you will be able to call upon them for guidance and to assist you by transferring their magickal and super-healing energies to you.

Mermaid healing energy

Once you're all charged up you will find that your healing abilities are enhanced, as the magickal mermaid energy pours out from the sacred shell symbol now embedded in your palm chakras. Powerful golden healing light (etheric) will stream through your hands as you place them upon yourself or your client, if you have a professional healing practice already. To prepare for a healing session:

- Play the sounds of the ocean waves on a CD, if you wish.

- Light a sea salt incense stick and some blue candles.

- Place seashells around the therapy couch or bed. Gently place the selected shells on your or your client's chakras and call in some powerful mermaid energy by saying:

> *Magickal beings from oceans and sea*
> *Lend me your powers, and assist me*
> *Show me the ailments and where to place shells*
> *Enhance my insight from the water of wells*
> *Healing of mermaids goes deep to the soul*
> *Health is restored, now fully whole.*

- Imagine a strong golden light coming out of your hands; this is the healing light of the mermaids.

- Place your hands on each shell in turn.

- In your mind, see the light pour through your hands into the shell and then through into the body as you focus on restored health on every level.

- As you work this way with the mermaids, you may find they pop visual details into your mind's eye concerning the healing, or they may give you messages through your feelings. Please don't ignore anything that comes up emotionally for you, as it could be a sign for yourself or for the person you are working on.

- When you have finished, carefully remove each shell. Imagine a large shell being placed around yourself of your client to keep the restorative and healing qualities intact and safeguarded.

- Drink a glass of water, and say:

> *I give thanks to the mermaids of oceans and sea,*
> *and accept this healing most graciously.*

Psychic protection

Whenever you work with magick it is vitally important that you protect yourself.

As a mermaid mystic you are most probably super sensitive, which means your empathetic nature is off the scale when it comes to drowning in others' energies. Wouldn't it be nice to keep all of your lovely energies to yourself, and not be weighed down by the negativity and harshness of others? Every day can be overwhelming for the would-be mermaid, and you need some form of spiritual protection in order to remain within your own positive energy field.

For psychic protection benefits, imagine yourself being encased in a beautiful, hard and enlarged seashell such as oyster, scallop or conch. Visualise the shell around you, protecting you against any harsh and lower energies that come your way. You can also retreat within its hard case when the going gets really tough! Add some bling to your shell by imagining a bright sparkling light of white around it, for uber protection.

Grounding

Before partaking in any spiritual work, whether it's meditation, invocation or any other form, you must ground yourself. This is not always easy for a mermaid mystic who would rather feel floaty than be attached to the earth, but even would-be mermaids need to be anchored within their bodies to keep connected to the earth realm instead of disappearing into another dimension! Going outside into nature and standing barefooted on the ground will instantly ground and connect you to the earth.

Imagine strong roots growing from the soles of your feet. Watch in your mind's eye as they bury deep into the ground, growing stronger and longer, until they reach the centre of the earth.

Visualise a crystal in the centre of the earth and let your roots wrap around it. Breathe up the crystalline energy, breathe up the earth magick and allow it surge through every part of your being. You are now grounded and ready to connect with mermaid magick.

Mermaid amulets

Amulets go back far into the ancient worlds and are found in nearly every culture to repel unwanted energies and bring about protection. Amulets are a focus point that leads you to affirm that which you believe they represent, thus aiding in amplifying their power. Whenever you look at them they enforce the energy of their purpose.

Amulets imbue the user with their associated powers of protection. For the mermaid mystic, shells are perfect for the job. Choose a shell for your own magickal protection and empowerment, then say the following protection incantation:

A circle around me of seashells and salt
Protect and safeguard me from any default
Amulets worn as mermaid's protection
Now safe to harness my magickal connection.

You may wish to craft the shell into the form of a ring, pendant or brooch to wear or simply keep it in your pocket, bra or hand when performing mermaid healing, magick or ritual.

Mermaid essence

Sometimes the natural mermaid in us can't quite handle the lower frequency of non-magickal people we find here on the land, which can lower your own energy and cause you to feel quite low and miserable. When those who refuse to open their hearts to the world of mermaids bring you down you need a quick fix to feel that mermaid thing going on.

Mermaid essences are the perfect solution for such occasions, and are very easy to make. You will need:

- 30 ml green-coloured bottle with a spray top
- ionised water
- essential oils such as eucalyptus, juniper or basil; this is my favourite combo for super connection with the mermaids, but feel free to experiment and choose your own
- tiny sea shells

Fill the bottle three-quarters of the way up with ionised water. You can buy this at a chemist, or simply use cold water that has previously been boiled. Add in a couple of drops of pure alcohol (cheap vodka works well). Add 20 drops of eucalyptus essential oil, 15 drops of basil oil and 12 drops of juniper oil. Sprinkle the tiny shells into the water. Twist the lid on tightly and shake the bottle.

Your mermaid essence is ready to spray into your aura, as a room clearing or healing space and for bringing in a vibration that is pure mermaid joy!

As you continue to work with the healing magick of the mermaids become aware of their energy, which refreshes, cleanses and renews your spirit. As you draw your bath, fill the kettle, skip over puddles and dance in the rain. Give thanks for the natural, cleansing, moist life-force properties that we and our beloved planet benefit from and survive because of.

Dive deep within and allow the healing magick to awaken your deepest emotions and stimulate your compassion, as you swim towards wholeness and the truth of your inner self.

High vibes

Keeping your vibration high and your chakras sparkly clean enables you to be more in tune with the messages the mermaids wish to convey to you. When you are a clear vessel it's easier to pick up the subtle guidance that the mermaids are trying to give you, as this can usually be on an emotional level. It's vitally important for you to distinguish the difference between your emotions and feelings and the messages you receive from the mermaids.

Mermaids are always trying to communicate with those who have the mer thing going on and wish for you to be the best you can possibly be. They may give you messages relating to:

- affairs of the heart
- seduction and feminine wiles
- revealing your true self
- prosperity and abundance
- emotions
- healing
- relationships
- psychic blocks
- healthy eating
- exercise
- drinking water
- meditation
- prayers and blessings

The uber sensitive mermaid mystic can expect to receive guidance through their feelings or emotions. This is known as **clairsentience**, meaning that you clearly feel intuitive information with your emotional or physical sense of feeling.

You may receive messages from the mermaids through a clear sense of seeing visions in your minds' eye, psychic dreams or relevant physical signs. This is known as **clairvoyance**.

If you have the gift of **claircognisance** the mermaids will download divine information into your mind, and you'll suddenly just know something without having learned it in the conventional way.

Clairaudience means you can hear the messages of the mermaids. These may come to you as voices of the mermaids in your mind, an external voice, through a song on the radio, overhearing a conversation that is relevant to you at the time or directly through another person.

Each of these intuitive senses corresponds to the body's chakra system. If you feel your psychic abilities need to improve or that you're out of balance on any level you can send beams of light to your chakras. For instance, if you're having an emotional wobble or problems with your love life, you can imagine an emerald green healing light beaming towards your heart chakra. Breathe the light in and see it cleansing and clearing away any blockages until your heart chakra is fully illuminated. You can work in this same way as you send the corresponding colours to each chakra in turn.

Mermaid waterfall of healing meditation

The mermaids work hard to keep the oceans from harm, and when pollution in any form disturbs the delicate equilibrium the mermaids send their powerful healing energy out to restore the balance. They work with us in the same way, and if our own ecosystem is clogged with the harshness of negativity or unhealthy consumption the mermaids offer to supercharge our chakras to bring about optimum health and psychic awareness.

It is time to visit the mermaid waterfall of healing to receive an energetic overhaul as the mermaids connect with you through the dimensions. Take a few deep breaths in and out, close your eyes and relax ...

You find yourself standing in front of a huge waterfall that cascades into a beautiful pool of the clearest water. As you peer in to check out your reflection seven mermaids appear from behind the waterfall, which has a shining crystal wall at its base. Each mermaid is drenched in individual colours, and together each mermaid makes up the colours of the rainbow.

Through the waterfall a mermaid who glows the deepest red beams this colour of light towards you. Your base chakra immediately fills with the brightest red as the colour rushes through you, expanding and healing this energy point that represents thoughts and feelings about safety, security and financial abundance. You are invited to make a wish that relates to any or all of these issues in your life. What do you wish to change? What do you want to bring into your life? As you make your wish a shaft of red light goes right through your base chakra area. So beautiful.

A mermaid who glows the brightest orange beams this colour of light towards your sacral chakra. Immediately you see this area fill with the brightest, luminescent orange as the colour rushes through you, expanding and healing this energy point that represents thoughts and feelings about addictions, appearance and creativity and how you think of yourself. You are invited to make a wish that relates to any or all of these issues in your life. What do you wish to change? What do you want to bring into your life? As you make your wish a shaft of orange light goes right through your stomach area. Breathe it in.

A mermaid who glows a golden yellow, like the sun, beams this colour of light towards your solar plexus chakra. Immediately you see this area fill with the brightest yellow as the colour rushes through you, expanding and healing this energy point that represents thoughts and feelings about personal power, will and control. You are invited to make a wish that relates to any or all of these issues in your life. What do you wish to change? What do you want to bring into your life? As you make your wish a shaft of yellow light goes right through your midriff area. Feel the power.

A mermaid who glows a deep emerald green beams this colour of light towards your heart chakra. Immediately you see this area fill with brilliant emerald green as the colour rushes through you, expanding and healing this energy point that represents thoughts and feelings about love, relationships, emotions and people attachments. You are invited to make a wish that relates to any or all of these issues in your life, and as you do a shaft of green light goes right through your chest. Relax.

A beautiful light blue mermaid flicks her tail and beams her light towards your throat chakra. You feel this area fill with the colour of sky blue as it rushes through you, expanding and healing this energy point that represents thoughts and feelings about speaking your truth, communication and creative expression. You are invited to make a wish that relates to any or all of these issues in your life, and as you do a shaft of bright blue light goes right through your neck. Breathe deeply.

A mermaid of deep indigo emerges and sends a light of the same colour towards your third eye chakra, in between your two physical eyes. Your forehead fills with a deep indigo blue, sparkles of white and flashes of silver that rush through you, expanding and healing this energy point that represents thoughts and feelings about wisdom, your future, the past, your desire to see through the veil and opening your spiritual sight. You are *invited to make a wish that relates to any or all of these issues in your life, and as you do a shaft of deep indigo blue goes right through your forehead. Allow any blockages to clear.*

A mermaid of royal purple beams this colour towards your crown chakra, at the top of your head. You immediately see this area fill with vivid royal purple as the colour rushes through you, expanding, cleansing and healing this energy point that represents thoughts and feelings about the creator, spirituality, divine guidance, knowledge and trust. You are invited to make a wish that relates to any or all of these issues in your life, and as you do a shaft of beautiful purple light goes right through the top of your head. Be the power.

Each chakra is perfectly cleansed and you feel this perfect rainbow of mermaid healing streaming through you from the base of your spine to the crown of your head. Breathe in the colours; feel the energy and the magick of the wishes that you have just made. The rainbow expands and you feel the energy of the mighty magickal mermaids before you.

You watch as a rainbow of colours swirls around the mermaids.

Shine brightly as the mermaids infuse your energy with healing and powerful magick that is divine love.

As you open your eyes, know that you have just received a most rejuvenating treatment at the mermaid waterfall of healing.

CHAPTER 5

MERMAID MOON MAGICK

Sarah Stilwell Weber 1911

Mystical moon of blessings and light
May deep your allurement open my sight
I call upon moonbeams to shine upon me
Reflecting the magickal flow of the sea.

Imagine floating in the dark ocean at the magickal time of midnight and gazing up at the shining stars as you bathe under the milky light of the moon. Perhaps it opens up a faint memory, a recollection for you upon magickal and ancient times …

The moon has always been a mystery to humankind and yet it fascinates us. Its soft, pale light seems to contain a magick all of its own, hinting at our celestial origins, which called to the souls of our ancestors who worshipped the moon phases as the triple goddess. Each phase of the moon represented her in three aspects of herself as:

- maiden: purity, youth, innocence
- mother: nurturing, growth, maturity
- crone: transformation, releasing, death

Magickal practitioners and mermaid mystics still respond to the moon in this way, for they believe in higher powers and higher energies and understand that everything in life is interconnected, is beyond separation.

The frequencies emanating from the moon affect our feelings and emotions, and its gravitational pull affects and controls the ebb and flow of the tides. During the new moon and full moon high tides are higher and low tides are lower than normal. During the first and last quarter moon, high and low tides are more moderate than normal.

The moon also rules the subconscious mind, and water is governed by the moon. Thus, of course, mermaids are naturally in tune with the moon and understand how its phases can affect human behaviour.

Because we humans are made up of at least 65% water we, like the tides, are affected by the pull of the moon, for it rules the flow of fluids. A woman's monthly menstrual cycle is affected in the same way, and her flow, ovulation and conception rates depend on the current phase of the moon. This is why it is often referred to as the 'moon time'!

The moon also affects our moods. We begin to withdraw, or go within, as the moon wanes, then are much more outgoing and have more energy when the moon waxes towards fullness. Centuries-old stories tell of men who turned into dangerous werewolves at the phase of a full moon. Remember that many truths are connected to stories of old. Did you know that police reports confirm there are more arrests for aggressive and outrageous behaviours around the phase of the full moon than at any other time of the month?

The moon really does determine how we behave, although this knowledge seems to have been lost through the mists of time. The power of the moon is no longer taken into consideration in this day and age unless you are magickal, of course, but it is true that we really are governed by it both emotionally and magickally.

Moon phases

Mermaid mystics should be acquainted with the phases of the moon as the power of spellwork and magick can be enhanced by working with them. It's important when working with mermaid moon magick to understand when the energy of the moon should be accessed and its transformational powers utilised.

Working with the correct phase of the moon to make magick will enhance the results of spellcasting. Each moon phase represents a magickal meaning and feminine energy, which can be used and called upon to assist spellcasting:

Phase	Goddess	Spells
New moon	Maiden	New projects, new beginnings, hope
Waxing	Maiden/mother of growth	Fertility, transformation
Full moon	Mother	Manifesting, desires, achievement, abundance
Waning	Mother/crone	Releasing, letting go, clearing
Dark moon	Crone	Banishment, deep wisdom, completion

Connecting with the magick of the mermaids in conjunction with the moon when casting spells will give an optimum result. The frequencies emanating from the moon affect our feelings, emotions and desires, all of which we can use to assist us when performing some mermaid moon magick. It is our subconscious, focus and intentions that inject the magickal outcome when used in conjunction with the correct moon phase for any given spell.

New moon	A fertile time for a new start. Wishes start to manifest as the moon waxes
Full moon	Very strong time to manifest your desires into being
Dark moon	For banishing and ridding yourself of what no longer serves

Mermaids really are best at bringing about all they desire, for this is how they grow and nurture all watery life. They wish to help us do the same.

The magickal phase of the full moon is a potent time for spellwork, for this is when magick abounds. Manifestation abilities are heightened as a magickal energy runs through all that you put focus on and vision into during the full moon.

Casting spells

Always have complete clarity as you focus on what you wish for, and remember to take into consideration any consequences that may occur to all living things as an outcome. Spells should be cast and wishes made with harm to none.

A spell is a powerful and sacred ritual of action that combines the use of magickal tools, symbols, elements and recipes with positive thoughts or words of intent, to create a powerful effect. Magickal spells are powered by personal positive energy, desire, belief, faith and emotion, and an awareness to cast a desired effect with unwavering focus and intent.

Mermaid moon magick harnesses and manipulates the energy of the moon and the magickal forces of the mermaids to bring about desires and wishes. Before casting a spell you must decide what the purpose of the spell is and be extremely clear about what it is you want.

Don't forget to always put in place protection for yourself. This could be a circle of white light around you, a physical circle of seashells that you've deliberately placed to stand within or imagining a seashell encasing you.

Magick needs personal powerful energy in order to work magnificently. Stand confidently in your power as you invoke the mermaids and the magick of the moon to ignite the magick of your spells.

Full moon manifestation spell

The full moon phase is when magick is at its optimum; it will charge you up with its natural powers.

As mermaids are strongly associated with the element of water they are also linked with the moon, which governs the ocean tides. Both the element of water and the moon have strong feminine energies that are receptive in nature, so mermaid magick is perfect to use to draw in the things you desire into your life, especially during a waxing and full moon.

- Light a white candle, hold a clear quartz crystal and face a full moon.

- Imagine you are standing within an oyster shell for protection.

- Say:

> *Mermaids of magick, mother of moon*
> *I ask that my wishes will come about soon*
> *Desires now placed in the crystal so clear*
> *Intentions now set, as I release fear*
> *Nurture growth until it's noon*
> *Giving thanks to the mystical moon*
> *Magick's strong, time to create*
> *and welcome unto me, my fate.*

- Place your intentions and desires into the crystal itself and leave it under the full moon until noon the following day, to charge and work with the moon's magickal properties in order to manifest that which you wish to bring into fruition.

- Blow the candle out and say:

> *This moon phasing spell is now made and done.*
> *With thanks to the mermaids, and with harm to none.*

Moonlight is reflected sunlight that is absorbed by the moon and then showered onto the earth as rays of luminous feminine energy that open your heart and your spiritual sight. This energy is vital for your balance and your health, for you are made up of the same vital minerals as the surface of the moon. So it's good to top up! Moon bathing is one way that you can do this. This doesn't necessarily mean putting on your bikini and lying out in your backyard in the middle of the night, but you could benefit from regular exposure to the moon. Just simply stand outside at night and look up to the moon to bathe your face in the restorative, feminine energy of its lustrous power, or if you're very brave go sky-clad (naked)!

On a metaphysical level the moon has always been looked upon as the keeper of magick and mystery, of intuition and wisdom. As you call down the moon she embraces you in her soft, luminous glow and assists in opening up your receptive feminine side. Never forget that the energy of the moon also lives within you, as it rules your emotions. Work in conjunction with the moon and be mindful of the phases that will affect you and all others. Remember, too, that when you embrace the law of analogy to understand the connection of all things you receive a supercharge of empowerment that connects you to the magick of the mermaids.

Calling down the moon

In witchy traditions, 'drawing down the moon' means invoking the goddess in order to channel her in a trance-like state. In mermaid moon magick we call down the moon to harness its magickal phase, and invite the mermaids in to guide and bestow us with their other-worldly powers.

The moon will guide the way as you swim towards enlightenment. Allow the mystical help of the mermaids to sprinkle you with magick as you and they work in conjunction with the moon on this fine night:

- Choose if you wish to be fully clothed, wearing swimwear or go sky-clad as you stand with your arms outreached to the moon and say:

> *I call down the moon this very night*
> *To shower within your soft pale light*
> *Replenish, cleanse me deep inside*
> *For 'tis where magick doth reside.*
> *I call down the moon this very eve,*
> *Whose mysticism and mystery together doth weave.*
> *Full power and magick bestow upon me*
> *As I connect with the mermaids of sea.*

- As you stand strong with your arms outstretched, a soft glow of moonlight will flood your face from above. Bathe in its soft, gentle energy as you become immersed in the divine feminine, which opens up your heart chakra like a beautiful rose. Feel any old habits, behaviours, fears and thought patterns that have been preventing you in moving forward fully dissolve.

- You are being given the presence of receptivity.

- As the moon streams its sacred light through the third eye in your forehead, picture clearly in your mind all that you would like to bring about.

- Allow the magickal workings of mermaid and moon enchantment to unfold as liquid moonlight fills you with qualities of intuition, integrity, peace, love, compassion, femininity, receptivity, confidence and a higher ability. Take a moment as these energies are assimilated into your very essence.

- Breathe deep, reflect and allow yourself to soak up the magick.

- Bathe in this way under the healing light for as long as you feel necessary and comfortable.

- Before you move back indoors say:

This mermaid moon magick is worked with harm to none.
So might it be. There, it is done.

Ancient civilisations used the moon to scry with and to predict weather patterns. They also noticed how nature is affected by the moon cycles: from the tides of the oceans to the emotions and behaviours of people and animals alike, the whole planet is affected by the moon in some way. The lunar phases of the moon rule over the growing of plants and herbs as well as providing appropriate times for spellcasting, and it is the mermaids who act as the facilitators of the moon to make magick.

Moon phases and hair

A mermaid's crowning glory is her hair (as well as her tiara, of course!), which can be enhanced through spellwork and moon magick. Brushing your hair by moonlight is a powerful process, especially while chanting a magickal incantation. As we've discovered already, hair is a very important magickal tool as well as giving us our individual look.

If you fancy a new do, make sure you adhere to the moon phases to get your new cut right:

- **Waning moon**: hair will grow slower if cut during the waning moon. Roots will strengthen and ends will not split.

- **Waxing moon**: hair will grow back quickly if cut during the waxing moon.

- **Full and new moon**: avoid cutting hair altogether at this time unless you want to grow your new style out at record speed.

For super-long mermaid hair, trim your ends (only a short amount) under a full moon, while chanting:

I trim my hair under the moon
My mermaid hair grows fast and soon
Let the length grow past my waist
So might it be, I am graced.

Essential oils contain magickal vibrations, and some have wonderful properties that when brushed through your hair will add gloss and an enchanting aroma. Try the following **moon luscious locks spell**.

Place some peppermint oil on your hairbrush, pull through your hair during a waxing moon phase and say:

Glossy hair is my wish
Luscious locks to flick and swish
Sacred oil within my brush
Stroke through slowly, there's no rush
Magick moon of waxing phase
My gratitude to you always.

For a **self-empowerment hair spell**, take hair that has collected in your hairbrush or comb.

Hold a red candle during a waxing moon and weave the hair carefully around it, saying:

Strength of flame and candle bright
Extinguish the dark that blacks out light
Release me of fears, worries and doubt
As I reclaim power with gusto and clout.

Light the candle, and allow it to burn all the way down.

Love and romance

Mermaids just love to help out with romance and any affair of the heart, for it is they who have instant access to the deep, swirling pools of emotions that is your heart chakra. Mermaids recognise that love is your true nature and it is necessary for you to honour the compassion you feel in your heart.

When you are true to yourself your light shines brightly with divine love, nourishing you from within and inspiring those around you. However, heart-break, loss and rejection can cause the heart chakra to shrink, and that's when you can become guarded and defensive. But fear not, for the mermaids wish for you to feel that love thing going on, so that you in turn become in love with love itself. And, of course, it raises you up to the highest levels of joy, which is the frequency where mermaids themselves reside.

If you wish to invite love and romance into your life or add some passionate zest back into a relationship, try casting this powerful but effective moon love spell under a full moon:

- Write the name of the one you love on a piece of paper, or leave it blank for your love to come in, and place it beneath a red or pink candle.

- Scatter rose petals in a circle around the candle.

- Face south (the magickal direction associated with love) and light the candle.

- Say:

> Mermaids of romance, bring me the one
> Invoking a love spell that can't be undone.
> As I light a candle, show me the ways.
> An image I see in the flame as I gaze,
> And draw on the essence full into my heart
> Wishing for love that is way off the chart.
> Desires, now shared, I wish to ignite,
> My passionate dreams so that I might,
> Attract beauty and love into my world.
> May deep the love mystery now be unfurled
> To bring about romance, kisses and laughter
> And be of my heart, happily ever after.

- Blow out the candle and direct the smoke of extinguished flame over your heart centre.

- Say:

> Gratefully I accept the magick of you,
> Grant love to assist in all that I do.
> Mermaids of romance, build passion in me
> Assist my transcendence. So might it be.

- Scatter the rose petals in a body of water such as a pond or bowl under the full moon and place the piece of paper under your pillow.

Sweet dreams!

Moon beauty spell

Mermaids are well known for their bewitching charm and alluring magnetism. They exude sexuality and promiscuity, which they revere as sacred and natural traits of the loving, feminine and soothing receptive properties of water. They naturally pass this potent life force onto us when we come into contact with them, helping us to feel good about ourselves and tapping into the magick of water.

Mermaids understand that all mermaid mystics enjoy all things beautiful and pretty, and like to look drop-down gorgeous most of the time.

Mermaids enjoy their own beauty magick routine, such a brushing their hair with a coral comb. They encourage you to harness nature for your beauty routines too and give you magickal tips, such as splashing your face in the magickal morning dew at dawn for its rejuvenation and youth-enhancing properties.

Sometimes you feel attractive, but the mermaids hear the ugly thoughts that criticise your perfect beauty. It is time to affirm some beauty to your life with the following moon beauty spell:

- Sit in front of your magick mirror at the magickal time of dusk at a new moon phase.

- Make a list of all of your redeeming features and qualities. Love them; appreciate them.

- Light a pink candle and say:

> *Mermaids surround me with magick of moon.*
> *Beauty abounds to come about soon.*
> *I look in my mirror of magick and gaze,*
> *At the flame-lit glass, which reflects quite a haze,*
> *I focus upon the belle in my heart,*
> *And draw from its essence; a beautiful start.*
> *Image appears, I see with new eyes*
> *Perception reveals attractive surprise!*

- As you feel the beauty expand within it will reflect back beautifully at you through the hearts and eyes of others, and of course through your magick mirror.

Dark moon banishment spell

Sometimes the mermaids need to protect their oceanic kingdom from dry land invaders, and will work with the magick of the dark moon to prevent anyone or anything over-swimming the boundaries. When your world becomes negatively affected by someone or something, it is time for a little banishment magick. The mermaids will flush out all forms of lower emotions that have been directed your way, such as jealousy, anger and resentment, and ward off any hurt that has been intended for you.

- Stand under a dark moon, preferably at the ocean or near a body of water (even if it's just a bowl of water).

- Light a black candle and say:

> *Beware! Be warned! Free me from harm*
> *Dark moon, be my magick charm*
> *Spite of tongue or curs-ed deed*
> *Now banished, ne'er to be received*
> *Trauma, grief, dispelled and drowned*

Mermaids' safety now abounds
Strong magick worked with harm to none.
So might it be. Now it is done.

- Let the candle burn down as you allow the energy of the dark moon to draw any lower energies from you.

- Say:

Protection in place, no need for fright
Healed and whole this very night.

Moon treasure spell

Many tales are told by those who have almost drowned in the oceans and seas, of how they were saved by mermaids who bestowed upon them a magickal kiss that enabled them to breathe underwater as the mermaid swam them safely to shore.

However, mermaids are also said to cause the destruction of ships and the drowning of sailors in order to retrieve sunken treasure chests crammed with pearls and gold and all kinds of precious jewels that mermaids just love to wear. These tales are perfect examples and representations of how unpredictable the ways of the oceans can be.

You can use these tales as metaphors to represent the searching for your own riches that lay dormant deep within yourself just waiting to be discovered.

If you are up to your neck and drowning in a sea of red demands, burying your head in the sand won't help you. Worry and stress can take their toll, so the mermaids are happy to help out with affairs of prosperity for they know that an abundance of treasures is your birthright. The universe always provides, and it is only through your human fearful thoughts and your belief in deficiency that you experience financial starvation.

Acknowledgement and taking responsibility of any debt is the first step and rule of mermaid magick when weaving a spell to become debt free. Try this moon treasure spell:

- Carve the figure of the sum of money you owe into a black candle.

- Carve the monetary amount you wish to earn into a green candle.

- Light them both under a dark moon and say:

To banish debt, light candle black
Dispel beliefs of less and lack
Debts reduced as candle burns
Green determines what one earns
Watch arrears melt away
Welcoming in a new pay day.

- Watch the black candle burn down, to banish debt completely.

Mermaid moon magick meditation

Now that you have cleared your debts it's time to reap the magick of prosperity that has been bubbling under the surface all along. You are invited to dive in to uncover the hidden treasure deep within, and reclaim your birthright of abundance as you swim towards your destiny.

Imagine you are standing on a cliff's edge at the magickal time of midnight. As the brightness of the full moon casts a shimmering silver hue upon you, the waves crash against the treacherous rocks below. As you look down, the dark waters of the unknown beckon to you. You can't resist, so you take the deepest breath in and dive down into the cool dark waters.

It is so refreshing as you swim down deeper and deeper, feeling more and more at ease with your surroundings, more familiar and relaxed as you swim further and deeper down to the depths of the ocean.

You feel your heart skip a beat as a mermaid swims towards you. With her long flowing tresses waving around her in the water, she takes you in her arms and holds you. Feelings of compassion and empathy overwhelm you as your heart chakra becomes healed and whole from unnecessary emotions, yours and others. You look up to gaze at her beautiful face in gratitude and she bestows you with a magickal mermaid kiss. You take a deep breath in and find that you can breathe easier than you ever do on land, as though you have been given gills.

The mermaid hands you a gift and points you towards some ancient ruins at the sea bed before disappearing. You notice pillars and an archway that you swim through. Suddenly you recognise the old and crumbling buildings that were once glorious but are now ancient. Have a good look around: swim in and out of the pillars, over the walls and around the old mosaic floors.

You swim through a doorway, a threshold that leads you into a dark cave — swim, swim —keep going until you see a glimpse of light. As the light gets brighter you find yourself in the most glorious seabed room decorated with the jewels of the sea, which sparkle and shimmer in the bright moonlight that filters down from the top of the ocean through an open hole in what was once a ceiling. You know this room; have a look around. Now you remember this is your room – the room where you received all those gifts, the abundance, the treasure, all part of your birthright. Take a moment and think back to then. Poseidon, Neptune – feel their energies, the energies of your family, your oceanic family!

You look down and see a trap door. Yes, this is it! Pull the handle, which releases the door easily. As you look down a huge old trunk floats up towards you. You grab it and put it beside you on the seabed.

Kneeling in front of it, you turn the key of the small lock at the front of the chest and open the lid. You gasp and then squint your eyes: the bright light that emanates from the chest is quite blinding.

Focusing your eyes, you now know why, for the chest is crammed with treasures of gold, diamonds, rubies and emeralds, tiaras, necklaces, bracelets and rings.

Have a look through – go on – seem familiar? This is wondrous, it is lavish!

This is your treasure! This treasure is your birthright. This treasure is and has always been yours. This treasure always will be yours.

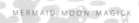

Tucked carefully underneath the lid is a golden envelope with your name on it.

Carefully open the envelope: it is from the great sea king himself, your father. It tells you of what is yours and how it always has been, but most of all it tells you of how you can access it right now and forever.

Read the note, for it is for your eyes only, after all.

After you've read the note, you put it back into the golden envelope and tuck it back in its place under the lid of the chest. Move the chest to the entrance of the trap door and see it lower gently in the water. This is your place, and you can come back at any time to read your letter and access your treasure at any time. In fact, all you have to do is see the chest in your mind's eye and absolutely know that all the treasure it contains comes easily to you. There is no way that it cannot, for it is your birthright; it fills your bank account, your purse and anywhere that you desire it to be.

You feel a new surge of energy sweep up through your tail, up through your body, up your face and out of the crown of your head, surrounding you entirely. It's electric; it is the magickal energy of abundance. The universe can only respond in one way now — and that is to match what you now have.

Feeling and knowing you are surrounded with riches, take a deep breath and swim out of the ancient ruins, through the pillared entrance and up and up and up through the cool clear waters, feeling refreshed, feeling alive and so abundant!

With a mighty push, you come to the surface and gasp as you feel the warm sun on your face.

With a smile and a new magickal energy surging through you, you continue to swim back to shore without looking back — knowing that you are rich in all ways and that the universe is absolutely supporting that.

When you are back on dry land, feel your feet upon the ground and take a deep breath.

Welcome back!

CHAPTER 6

SPREAD THE MAGICK

HERBERT COLE ·1915·

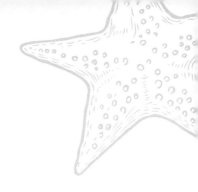

~\⁄~

Rescued from a dark abyss
Awakened with a mermaid kiss
Your mermaid soul stirs from the deep
Treasure is your gift to keep
New life beckons, old fear fades
Spread the magick of mermaids.

~⁄\~

As we have discovered, mermaids are the magick behind the ebb and flow of the oceans and seas and of water itself. It is time to embrace the tranquillity and enchantment of their world and integrate it with our everyday lives.

Treat every day as though you are starring in your own mermaid movie. Remember that the mermaids feel your emotions, so share with them your joy, laughter and passion and have fun. As you honour and work magickally with the mermaids, they will impart to you mermaid wisdom and magickal tips as they capture your imagination.

Everyday mermaid magick

Make every day a magickal mermaid day:

- Start the day by pulling a mermaid oracle card to receive an insightful and in-depth message.

- Revive your spirit and relax in a sea salt bath.

- Lay seashells upon your chakra points for some mermaid energy healing.

- Be seductive and embrace your feminine wiles.

- Start swimming regularly at your local pool. If you can't stand the chlorine (and let's face it, what mermaid enjoys bleach on her scales?), find a natural pool or river where it's safe to swim or swim or paddle in the ocean.

- Eat healthy mermaid food, such as seaweed and kelp.

- Meditate on a beach.

- Collect litter from the shore and coast lines.

- Make mermaid wishes.

- Leave out little mermaid gifts.

- Gaze into your magick mirror.

- Brush your hair purposefully.

- Sing and dance.

- Carry mermaid crystals.

- Wear shell jewellery.

- Praise the rain.
- Bless every glass of water you drink

Remember that whenever you drink, bathe in or are in close proximity to water, become conscious of the undines and acknowledge them for working hard behind the scenes.

Mermaids need you!

The mermaids are very real and this blue planet cannot exist without them, for water is our life source. For too long the spirits of water have been dishonoured and dismissed. Humankind has tried to do things their way and, instead of leaving nature to do its thing naturally, has attempted to speed up the process by using man-made chemicals that are literally preventing the mermaids from doing their job well and effectively. Water is suffering as oceans are being filled with poisons that are killing the natural habitat of the seas.

Mermaids are fighting to keep the oceans clean and clear of pollution from shipping, as well as from eroding soil during rainstorms. Much of this run-off flows to the sea, carrying with it agricultural fertilisers and pesticides. Eighty per cent of pollution to the marine environment comes from small sources from the land, such as septic tanks and motor oil. The ever-increasing popularity of cruising is contributing to vast human waste being dumped into the depths of the ocean, suffocating marine life including the beautiful colourful coral reefs, which are fading to a world of grey.

Huge cruise liners now rule the oceans and desecrate the waves with an excessive amount of pollution from the thousands of passengers who holiday on our oceans. And, of course, there are the evils of plastic, which are literally strangling, deforming and killing the innocent marine life that swallows or gets caught up in carelessly thrown bottles and bags.

How much longer can this incredible kingdom of water survive, until the natives of land step in and put a stop to the mindless destruction? It is time to seriously help the mermaids through physical measures that will prevent pollution by supporting clean-up groups such as oceana.org or by visualising clean and pure waters across the globe.

All is not lost. Those who are awakening to the conch call of the mermaids can feel their mystic self stir from the depths within. Glimmers of ancient memories surface, recalling moonlight bathing in deep blue pools, floating in midnight waters under the magick of the stars and experiencing the pure delights of diving beneath the waves, connecting to the soul mystery that is the lost world of Atlantis. To the mermaids it was only yesterday when they played with you, my friend. They miss you and the magick you exude when you allow yourself be the free spirit of the seas that you naturally are.

The world has changed and seems to spin at a much faster pace, with high-tech gadgets and transport. To embrace the kingdom of the seas does not mean you have to lose all that you've acquired in this day and age. When you recognise that the mermaids are the magick beings behind all that is alive in the bodies of water that cover two-thirds of this planet and who work in conjunction with the moon and your own emotions, you yourself are brought back into alignment with the natural world. In turn you will find that your own powerful manifestation and healing abilities are ignited, enabling you to change how you experience life as you embrace the magick that is within and all around. That is the way to bring the oceans and the world back into balance.

The mermaids, the spirits of water, are waiting in the waterfalls, streams and lakes. They wait for you in the seas and oceans. They are present in every drop of water, from puddles to baths. Will you not acknowledge them as you bathe, cleanse and drink, and take a step sideways to become part of their magick? The true mermaid mystic flips her tail between the world of water and that of land, for she knows and is part of the reality and magick of both.

It is time to introduce one of those worlds that has been hidden for too long now into the other that has seemed to have lost its way without its magickal counterpart. Sixty-five per cent of our body is made up of the basic element of water, and water cannot exist without the presence of a water spirit. This means that we all have the energy of the mermaids within us!

It is time to honour the mermaid within and to harness the natural magick of the mermaids, which you can tap into at any time the moment you remember who you really are.

It is time to honour the oceanic kingdom with which you are naturally connected from the very depths of your soul, by becoming a magickal defender of the seas.

It is time to supercharge your life with *mermaid magick*!

Ocean healing spell

The mermaids are calling you to help clean up the pollution that has infected not only their world but also that of all living beings that inhabit the seas and oceans – and of course the water itself. If you are feeling the call and would like to assist, here is a simple but effective healing spell the mermaids will receive well. You will need:

- a bowl of water
- sea salt
- mermaid crystals, seashells and stones
- 1 gold candle
- paper and pencil
- optional: a CD of the sound of waves, seaweed, incense

Face the magickal direction of west and place the bowl of water in front of you.

Add in a few pinches of natural sea salt and some mermaid crystals and seashells to the water.

Imagine yourself encased in a shell or see yourself within a circle of white light. Ignite the candle, place it on your mermaid altar and say:

Spirits of water, mermaid in me
I offer to help heal all beings of sea
May the waters be cleansed to whole purity
Let the clearing begin, so might it be.

Tear the paper into small pieces. On each piece write a word of healing that the ocean would benefit from, such as: clear, whole, pure, healed, revitalised, energised, beauty, purified. Wrap each piece of paper individually around a shell, crystal or stone and submerge them in the water. Imagine the oceans receiving the healing gifts that the words represent.

Bring your focus to the flame of the candle, and watch the golden/ orangey light flicker on top of the golden wax.

Using intention, send a golden light to the water in the bowl. See in your mind's eye the water receiving this blast of high vibrational heal- ing light and intend this for all the oceans and seas. As this is received, the mermaids offer their energy to take this light out across the world to heal and regenerate all bodies and its inhabitants of water across the globe.

When you know in your heart that it is done, blow out the candle and say:

By the power of water, of ocean and sea
With thanks I return, so might it be.

Oceans of blessings . . .

IMAGE CREDITS

Chapter openers: Knüpfer, B. 1892, *Duel of the Tritons*, Christies https://www.christies.com/lotfinder/paintings/benes-knupfer-duel-of-the-5787616-details.aspx

Page 2: Stratton, H. 1899, *The fairytales of Hans Christian Andersen*, Wikisource, https://en.wikisource.org/wiki/The_Fairy_Tales_of_Hans_Christian_Andersen_(Stratton)/The_Little_Mermaid#/media/File:Page_126_illustration_b_in_fairy_tales_of_Andersen_(Stratton).png

page 30: Krasivo, N. *Beautiful young mermaid sitting on a stone*, Shutterstock https://www.shutterstock.com/image-vector/beautiful-young-mermaid-sitting-on-stone-1064436335?studio=1

Page 56: Ford, H.J. 1904, *The mermaid and the boy*, Flickr, https://www.flickr.com/photos/eoskins/15649158938/in/album-72157642934795443/

Page 73: Bauerle, A. circa 1800, *Mermaid swimming with a child*, Flickr https://www.flickr.com/photos/sofi01/6355697671/

Page 76: Robinson, C. 1899, *The Little Mermaid*, Flickr https://www.flickr.com/photos/eoskins/27442231512

Page 87: Furian, P. *Seven main chakras*, Shutterstock https://www.shutterstock.com/image-vector/seven-main-chakras-beaded-along-corresponding-194952908?studio=1

Page 101: Outhwaite, I. cira 1900, *Mermaid*, Trzcacak https://www.trzcacak.rs/imgm/iTxhJTw_ida-rentoul-outhwaite-elves-and-fairies/

Page 106: Weber, S. 1911, *Mermaid mother and child*, Flickr, https://www.flickr.com/photos/eoskins/29039608043/

Page 134: Cole, H. 1915, *Mermaid*, British Museum www.britishmuseum.org/research/collection_online/collection_object_details.aspx?objectId=738421&partId=1&searchText=herbert+cole&people=128905

ABOUT THE AUTHOR

Best-selling author Flavia Kate Peters is known as the Fairy Seer who embraces the magickal path of the old ways and that of fairy-craft. A teacher of natural and ancient magick, Flavia is the founder of the Mermaid Energy Healing System® and trains others through her professional certification courses and is a regular presenter on the mind-body-spirit and pagan circuits. Television appearances include *Celebrity Haunted Hotel* and *Lightworker's Guide to the Galaxy*, along with various guest slots for BBC Radio. She regularly graces the pages of *Spirit and Destiny* magazine and is a columnist for the magazines *FAE* and *Witchcraft & Wicca*. Her authentic and honest approach make her a most sought-after wisdom keeper.

www.flaviakatepeters.com